Mr. Andy Caldwell
Dear Andy!
God Bless you for your
efforts to defend our
Republic!

ROBERT MUELLER
ERRAND BOY FOR THE NEW WORLD ORDER

John Milkovich
February 20, 2019

JOHN MILKOVICH

Robert Mueller
Errand Boy for the New World Order

Book Orders directed to:
John Milkovich
656 Jordan
Shreveport, LA
318-425-1957
www.robertmuellererrandboy.com

Printed in the United States of America.
1st Edition September 2018
1st Printing September 2018

Dedicated to Mark and Lura Milkovich
For their long lives of doing the Right thing.

In Memoriam
Charles McKee (1948-1988)
Major, United States Army
Dr. David M. Graham, DDS (1939-2006)
Captain, United States Air Force

<u>Acknowledgements</u>

Many have made invaluable contributions to this work. They include John Jeremy Long, III. This author, and millions of Americans, are indebted to Dr. Jerome Corsi, Ph.D., for his trenchant insights expressed in *Killing the Deep State.*

And all Americans are in the debt of the courageous federal agents, writers, researchers, officials and ordinary citizens who have risked all, and sacrificed much, to bring to light governmental wrongdoing of the last 30 years.

CONTENTS

__Foreword__

"He's a bad guy, going all the way back." So, someone recently told me about Robert Mueller in a moment of extemporaneous, parking-lot politics, the kind that are endemic to the American experience.

The comment about Mr. Mueller followed several observations: Mueller had essentially told Congress that a Surveillance State was necessary in America, because it was needed to prevent another 9-11; Mueller made this statement even though top Government and Intelligence Officials had been repeatedly warned before 9-11 about imminent terrorist attacks; 9-11 could have been prevented if executive brass had simply heeded and responded to the repeated warnings of rank and file federal agents; Mueller basically lied to Congress, telling members of the Legislative Branch, that the Government and Intelligence had no forewarnings of 9-11.

And the parking lot pundit followed his comment that "He's a bad guy, going all the way back," with this observation: "If no one knew about 9-11, why did insiders make a bunch of money on the stock market by the investments they made right before the attack?"

The commentator was intelligent, and not manacled by formal education. And in fact, he was right. Mr. Mueller has been a "bad guy, going all the way back." Thirty years back.

And yes, pre-9-11 investments that specifically depended upon the disastrous events of 9-11 in order to succeed, were made, on a massive scale, by establishment insiders, shortly before the attack.

The parking-lot pundit's remarks were as accurate as they were unadorned. And they raise salient questions. The man on the street, by perusal of the abundant documentation uncovered by independent researchers, is able to decipher that Mueller has been corrupt for decades.

Why then have many in the mainstream media ignored these egregious excesses? Is it because many in the mainstream media are incapable of studying the historical and documentary record? Are they unwilling to research the basic sources, witness testimonies, documentaries and books? Or are the mainstream media controlled by a financial elite that is horror-struck at the thought that Mueller's perfidy might be exposed? Are the political and economic powers behind the Media Masque terrified that the exposure of Mueller's mercenary methods could cause Mueller's concerted attack on the Presidency to unravel?

While important questions remain, several facts are clear. Based on the historical, documentary and evidentiary record, Mueller has functioned as both the architect of, and willing accomplice to, governmental corruption and coverups "going all the way back" at least 30 years. And Robert Mueller has taken clear aim at the Presidency of the 45th President of the United States, Donald J. Trump.

Robert Mueller was asked, through email to his spokesman, Peter Carr, to answer questions, or comment, about his past work as a member of the Department of Justice and the FBI. The author received no substantive reply.

This is a Book that, on its face, purports to be about official corruption. And indeed, it is. It is also a Book about Heroes. Events from the last 30 years reflect unfavorably upon some intelligence agents and officials, and upon some media executives and reporters. However, as a distinctly American Narrative, the journey of the last 30 years is also peopled with researchers, writers and intelligence agents, who took great risks, and made supreme sacrifices, to bring the truth to light.

Dr. David M. Graham, DDS, encountered four Middle Eastern men in Shreveport, Louisiana, in the fall of 2000, whose conduct was highly suspicious. Graham suspected they were planning to make a terrorist attack on Barksdale Air Force Base, an American nuclear installation, situated in Bossier City, Louisiana across the Red River from Shreveport. Graham reported the men and their problematic conduct to federal agents in Shreveport in November 2000.

Graham was stunned— and outraged— on October 5, 2001, some three and one-half weeks after 9-11, when he saw the cover story picturing the 19 hijackers involved in the attack of 9-11. On the front page, among the hijackers, were two men Graham had met in Shreveport— and reported to federal agents, ten months before 9-11. Graham was poisoned on the verge of publishing a book that set out what he saw and heard— and what he told federal authorities.

David Graham is one hero.

There are others, including those whose sacrifices for Justice have not yet been discovered, whose stories have not yet been told, whose heroism has not yet been lauded.

Robert Mueller is an imposing and dangerous figure, whose temporal power rises like a mist from the subterranean enclaves of the occult elite.

Yet, despite Mueller's methods, his furies and his menacing power, the American Narrative continues.

John Milkovich
Shreveport, Louisiana
September 5, 2018

Chapter 1

Tributes, Trajectory and Treason

The mainstream media has been almost uniformly monochromatic in its depiction of Robert Mueller. Mueller was appointed by Deputy Attorney General Rod Rosenstein on May 17, 2017, to serve as Special Counsel and lead the investigation into alleged "Russian Collusion" by President Trump. Mueller, the mass media tells us, is the very picture of probity, propriety and public service. In fact, both mainstream Journalists and prominent public officials have seemingly engaged in a frantic competition to outdo each other, in heaping plaudits on Mr. Mueller.

As writer Phil Gibbons notes, after Mueller's appointment as special counsel, "From both sides of the aisle came praise for Mueller, the former FBI director with an alabaster image." In an Article entitled "Finally something Democrats and Republicans agree on: Former FBI director is right pick for special counsel," the *Washington Post* reported on May 17, 2017, that Mueller's appointment was an event "sparking a rare moment of bipartisanship on Capitol Hill." Said North Carolina Senator Richard Burr, "having someone like Bob Mueller head the investigation assures the American people that there's no undue influence . . . ." Grant Woods, former Arizona Attorney General, implored Congress to "Let Robert Mueller finish the job that he is unquestionably qualified to do." Paul Charlton, former U.S. Attorney for the District of Arizona, declared that "putting someone like Bob Mueller in charge of this prosecution should give our public even greater confidence." Wrote William G. Otis, in *USA TODAY*, on June 14, 2017, "Robert Mueller is a man of integrity with a long record of public service."[1]

However, there is an epic disconnect between the Robert Mueller described by the Mass Media and Officialdom as a model of public propriety, and the Robert Mueller, documented by independent researchers: a chronic Collaborator, with a career characterized by cover-ups, corruption and unconscionable conduct— an ever-willing instrument of Deep State dissimulation.

As researcher Kevin Ryan writes,

> What some people don't know about Mueller is that he has a long history of leading government investigations that were diversions or cover-ups. These include the investigation into the 1988 bombing of Pan Am Flight 103, the investigation into the terrorist financing Bank of Credit and Commerce International (BCCI), and the FBI investigations into the crimes of September 11th, 2001.[2]

As writer, Barbara Boyd, declares, the plaudits to Mueller for "reorganizing the FBI" to become effective in "counterintelligence and counterterrorism . . . in the wake of 9/11" is "Washington D.C. public relations claptrap. The FBI under Mueller excelled at entrapping the otherwise innocent, and constructing a surveillance state strongly resembling that portrayed by George Orwell in the novel, 1984."[3] Mueller's career, she states, constitutes a "trail of prosecutorial misconduct."[4] "In reality," she concludes, Mueller "is about as corrupt as they come, bending and twisting the law every which way necessary to serve the goals of those who provide him assignments."[5]

As Benjamin Wittes and Susan Hennesey have written, "Don't be fooled by Mueller's Boy Scout act."[6] "Mueller is so political that he's spent his entire career going back and forth between politicians."[7] Moreover, the mantra that Mueller does not specialize in leaks— media manipulation— is a façade, a cover story: "Sure, Mueller's got a rep for rarely speaking in public or giving interviews. But behind the scenes he's obviously spending day and night dishing dirt on Donald Trump . . . to any reporter who will listen."[8]

And he is mercenary in his methods. As Sean Hannity protested on August 20, 2018, Mueller operates on one of the basic premises that was used by Stalin's Chief of Police, Lavrentiy Beria: "Show me the man, I will show you the crime."[9] As Hannity observed, "Those are chilling words, and the opposite of how the American justice system is supposed to operate. Our system is designed to prosecute crimes, not persecute individuals we disagree with."[10] As another commentator has noted, "[Mueller] is in the game to charge some Trump associate, if not Trump himself, with anything he can think of."[11]

Mueller has left his imprint on some of the most notorious episodes of government wrongdoing of the last thirty years.

Chapter 2

Whitey Bulger Gang

James "Whitey" Bulger's reign as the "murderous boss of Boston's notorious Winter Hill Gang, also known as the Irish Mafia"[12] from 1975 to 1994, was documented by William F. Jasper, of *The New American,* among others. The U.S. Attorney's Office and FBI Office in Boston protected Bulger and his gang. In the midst of Bulger's homicidal heyday, Mueller served as Assistant U.S. Attorney and later U.S. Attorney for Boston.

The Boston FBI used Bulger and his associates as confidential informants; protected Bulger and his gang from prosecution; took bribes from Bulger; and gave Bulger's cohort timely tip-offs on law enforcement investigations, to enable Bulger and his cadre to evade investigation, arrest and prosecution. According to some researchers, the Boston FBI assisted Bulger's gang in the commission and coverup of murders.

In pretrial hearings in May 1997, Whitey Bulger's lieutenant, Stephen "Stevie" Flemmi, "The Rifleman,"

> dropped a bombshell, claiming immunity from the criminal charges due to his status as a confidential informant for the FBI. According to Flemmi, he and Bulger had been cooperating with the FBI for decades and had been told by their FBI handlers they could do anything short of 'clipping someone' without fear of prosecution.[13]

As uncovered by Kevin Cullen of *The Boston Globe*, FBI Agent John Connolly was Bulger's "corrupt handler";[14] FBI Supervisor John Morris was Connolly's "corrupt supervisor."[15] Agents John Connolly and John Morris— Bulger's "protectors"— "would tip him off to investigations and wiretaps by other police agencies."[16] Thus, "Time after time, Massachusetts state and local police had their elaborate, years-long investigations of Bulger foiled by FBI interference."[17] As independent journalist Sara Carter has similarly observed, "Connolly went out of his way to protect Bulger and aided the crime boss against investigations being conducted by the Boston PD and the Massachusetts State Police. . . . Connolly would inform Bulger of wiretaps and surveillance being conducted by law enforcement."[18] Moreover, "the same FBI sources had earlier tipped the duo [Bulger and Flemmi] about bugging and wiretap efforts of the Boston police in 1980 and the Drug Enforcement Agency (DEA) in 1984."[19] Further, "It was the FBI, says Flemmi, who tipped him and Bulger about the imminent arrest plans by state authorities in 1995."[20]

Thus, FBI Agent John Morris was the Supervisor of FBI Agent John Connolly, who was in turn the "handler" of Whitey Bulger. Morris admitted under cross examination, in the late '90s, that "he had exchanged Christmas gifts of books and liquor with Bulger and Flemmi. He also confessed to taking upwards of $6,000 from Bulger. And yes, Morris testified, he and other agents had shielded the mobster duo from prosecution for 20 years."[21] Further,

> On June 3, 1997, federal prosecutors disclosed, under an order by Judge [Mark L.] Wolf, that Bulger was indeed an FBI informant for much of the time period relating to the indictment which charges Bulger and four other defendants

. . . with coordinating the criminal activities of the Winter Hill Gang . . . of the New England branch of La Cosa Nostra— the Mafia."[22] As William F. Jasper of *The New American* summarized on March 22, 2018, "For two decades (1975-1994) Bulger led a charmed existence, as his brutal gang carried out their crime rampage *under the FBI's protection.*[23]

More daunting than the protection of the Bulger gang by the Boston FBI and the U.S. Attorney's Office, according to a 1998 report by *The New American,* "are the revelations and charges that the FBI officials involved may have winked at— if not actually assisted beforehand, or covered up afterwards— more than one of the Winter Hill Gang's 'clippings.'"[24]   As *The Boston Globe*'s Kevin Cullen reported in 2011, "When they weren't pocketing bribes from Bulger, [FBI Agents Connolly and Morris] were helping him murder potential witnesses who were poised to expose the FBI's sordid, Faustian deal with the rat named Whitey Bulger."[25]

Jai Alai is a Basque-originated sport, in some respects resembling racket ball. Jai Alai is played with a wicker basket-type racket called a cesta, generates ball speeds up to 180 mph, endangers the athletes that play it— and spawns millions of dollars in international gambling.

In 1981, the Oklahoma-based owner of World Jai Alai, Roger Wheeler, was murdered, after he found out that money was being skimmed from his operation. The culprits? Whitey Bulger's Winter Hill Gang. Within a few months, Brian Halloran, hit man for the Bulger Gang, turned informant and went to the FBI with inside information. John B. Callahan had owned World Jai Alai before Wheeler did. Halloran informed the FBI that Bulger; Bulger's Lieutenant, Stephen "Stevie" Flemmi; and mob-connected, former World Jai Alai owner, Callahan, had offered to pay Halloran to kill Wheeler. Halloran offered to testify against Bulger, Flemmi and Callahan, and he asked for protection under the federal Witness Protection Program.

The FBI rejected Halloran's offer to provide evidence against Bulger and Flemmi. Someone leaked that Halloran had "tried to snitch"[26] on Bulger and Flemmi. A few weeks later, Halloran and a friend were shot to death outside a Boston pub.

In July 1982, two months after Halloran's murder, homicide detectives from Tulsa and the State Police from Connecticut and Massachusetts "descended on Boston in a search for John Callahan, in connection with the Wheeler murder."[27] The detectives met with the federal organized crime strike force prosecutor, Jeremiah O'Sullivan. Callahan was not only a prime suspect in Roger Wheeler's murder. Callahan was also a potential witness against Bulger and Flemmi for their part in the murder of Roger Wheeler. However, in August 1982, a few weeks after homicide investigators from three states converged on Federal Prosecutor O'Sullivan in Boston to locate John Callahan and pursue leads on the murder of Roger Wheeler, Callahan's bullet riddled body was found stuffed in the trunk of Callahan's Cadillac in a Miami airport parking garage. *The New American* opined that "Bulger and Flemmi were tipped that Callahan had become a major liability."[28]

In May of 1998, detectives from Oklahoma, Florida and Connecticut spoke with Ed Bradley of *60 Minutes*. The detectives let Bradley know that they were angered that the Boston FBI stonewalled their investigation; failed to inform them of Halloran's inside information about the murder of Roger Wheeler— and apparently leaked Halloran's identity and incriminating knowledge to the Boston-based mobsters. Their concern was that federal authorities in Boston had informed Bulger's cohort that Halloran was willing to testify against them, and that Bulger's gang may have killed Halloran because of that leak from the Feds.

Sergeant Mike Huff of the Tulsa Police Department averred that the conduct of the Boston FBI in covering up key evidence about the murder of Roger Wheeler constituted obstruction of justice. Roger Wheeler's son, David, was more blunt in his statements to *60 Minutes:*

> We've discovered that all along the FBI has been in bed with the prime suspects in my father's murder . . . . They not only protected my father's killers, they, to this day, are protecting my father's killers. And they are, to this day, withholding information from the police. This is 18 years of covering up a crime. This is 18 years of being an accessory to murder.[29]

What's more, the mob hit on former World Jai Alai owner, Roger Wheeler, was, *The New American* observes, "likely assisted by Paul Rico,"[30] a former Boston FBI Agent who retired from the Bureau, went to work at World Jai Alai, and was later indicted for helping Bulger plan Wheeler's murder. As Boston writer, David Boeri reports, Rico died in jail after being charged with committing the murder of Wheeler with Bulger and Stephen Flemmi.[31]

Earlier in 1965, Boston man, Teddy Deegan, was killed. According to *The New American,* "The [Boston] FBI and [Department of Justice] DOJ framed . . . four scapegoats [for the murder], who were then sent to prison."[32] Three of the four men were sentenced to die in the electric chair. The reason the Feds framed potentially innocent people? As Sara Carter has reported, "[T]he bureau buried the truth to protect Vincent "Jimmy" Flemmi, their informant, who was the brother of Stevie Flemmi, a partner of Bulger."[33]

Of the four men convicted for the murder of Teddy Deegan, two died in prison. At least one of the four, Louis Greco, was posthumously proven innocent— after he died in prison. In 2001, the four men were exonerated of Deegan's murder. In 2007, a jury awarded over $101 million in damages to the surviving victims and the families of the deceased— a reparation ultimately paid for by the American taxpayer.

In the 1980s, Mike Albano, then a member of the Massachusetts Parole Board, became convinced that the Boston FBI and DOJ had used bogus evidence to frame the four men for the murder of Teddy Deegan. In 1983, after he indicated that he might vote to release one of the men, Albano was visited by Bulger's FBI handlers— John Morris and John Connolly. Mike Albano stated, "They told me that if I wanted to stay in public life, I shouldn't vote to release a guy like Limone"[34]— one of the four convicted men. Stated Albano, "They intimidated me."[35] After Albano was elected Mayor of Springfield, Massachusetts, the FBI retaliated against him. Albano "soon found the FBI hot on his tail, investigating his administration for corruption. The FBI took down several people in his administration, and Albano is convinced that the FBI wasn't interested in public integrity as much as in publicly humiliating him because he dared to defy them."[36]

10

The FBI not only tried to intimidate a public official who disagreed with the conviction of one or more of those charged for the murder of Teddy Deegan. The FBI also devastated the family of at least one man wrongly convicted of the murder.

Louis Greco, of the Revere Neighborhood of North Boston, was decorated with two Bronze Stars and a Purple Heart for his valor in World War II. Greco was a promising prize fighter before the War. As Boston writer, David Boeri, reported, Greco came back from Europe a war hero, with his 6th grade education, war injuries, "a shattered ankle and no future in the ring."[37] He "sold his muscle as an enforcer and worked as a repo man,"[38] seizing vehicles for which payments were overdue. But when it came to Revere, a longtime friend attested, "he would do anything for people here."[39]

In 1967, Greco had been convicted for murdering a "small-time hoodlum . . . Teddy Deegan in a Chelsea alley"[40] in Boston— and sentenced to death. At the time Greco was sent to prison in 1967, he had a wife 20 years younger than himself, and two sons, Louis, Jr., 13 years old, and Edward aged 11.

Greco was convicted on the basis of the testimony of a Boston mobster, Joe "The Animal" Barbozo. One of Barbozo's FBI handlers, Paul Rico, was later implicated, along with the Whitey Bulger gang, in the 1982 murder of Roger Wheeler. Barbozo's crucial trial testimony implicated Louis Greco as the triggerman, who slew Teddy Deegan in an alley in the Chelsea neighborhood of Boston.

In 1970, Barbozo admitted to Boston Journalist James Southwood, "Louis Greco wasn't in the alley."[41] Barbozo thus recanted the testimony used to convict Louis Greco. Journalist Southwood reported the recantation of Barbozo's vital testimony to Barbozo's FBI handlers, including Rico, to the then U.S. Attorney and to the Suffolk County District Attorney whose office prosecuted the case against Greco.

Greco passed at least eight different lie detector tests administered by outside experts, which indicated that he was truthful when he stated he wasn't in the Chelsea alley in 1965 when Teddy Deegan was murdered, and didn't shoot Deegan. Moreover, evidence indicated he wasn't even in Massachusetts at the time of the killing— he was living in Florida. Greco had been spared the electric chair when Massachusetts abolished the death penalty. Still, Greco died in prison in 1995. Judicial exoneration came later, in 2007.

At the Civil Trial for Greco's wrongful conviction in 2006, Louis Greco's younger son, Edward, testified that after his father was imprisoned, his mother drank heavily and neglected to feed him and his brother or wash their clothes. His mother often beat him. As David Boeri reported, Edward testified at trial that,

> [w]ithin a year or so of Greco's imprisonment, [Greco's wife] stopped visiting her husband in prison. She brought another man in the house with her children. Then one day in 1970, she abandoned them without notice and took off for Las Vegas with the savings bonds Edward had gotten for his birthdays and his paper route money, as well.[42]

Louis Greco was "outraged that a mother could do that to her own children"[43]— but powerless in prison to do anything about it.

12

Reported Boeri, "After his father died in prison in 1995, [elder son, Louis Jr.] drank a can of Drano and died."[44] Louis Greco's younger son, Edward,

> often without a home and unable to go to college as he once planned, became a junkie. By the time he was 20, he lived in a state prison. Edward went to New Orleans after his release, fought a battle against heroin and cocaine, pulled things together, and then fell apart again after his father died, he told the court in 2006. He had a bad heart, lost a lung and his spleen, was living in a nursing home, and had recently been living at the Salvation Army.[45]

Edward Greco died of an overdose in 2010 within a few days of receiving his portion of the judgment for his father's wrongful imprisonment. His mother didn't attend his funeral.

As Boeri reported, Louis Greco "had been the glue that held his family together, Edward testified at the civil trial in 2006."[46] James Southwood was the venerable, old school Boston journalist who covered the Louis Greco case for 40 years, and heard Joey Barbozo, the star witness that falsely implicated Greco in the murder admit, years later: "Louis Greco wasn't in the alley." Stated James Southwood, "What happened to Louie destroyed those kids."[47]

"In 1994, Bulger was tipped off by his FBI handler John Connolly that investigators were closing in on him. He went on the lam and eluded capture for 16 years."[48] Ultimately, Bulger was arrested in California in 2011— when the wrongdoing of Bulger and the Boston Feds was a potential issue in Robert Mueller's reappointment in 2011 as head of the FBI. Bulger was tried in 2013; convicted of 31 counts, including 11 murders; and sentenced to two consecutive life sentences, plus 5 years.

The Boston FBI supposedly used Bulger and Flemmi to "give up their pals in the Mafia," noted Kevin Cullen in 2011.[49] "The problem with [this FBI strategy] is that it didn't take into account that the most vicious, murderous gangsters in Boston were Whitey Bulger and Stevie Flemmi."[50]

Where was Robert Mueller during Whitey Bulger's reign of Terror? During the Boston FBI's treacherous duplicity, and apparent complicity in murder? Geographically and temporally, at least— he was right in the middle of it. From 1982 through 1985, Mueller worked as an Assistant U.S. Attorney in Boston for the District of Massachusetts, and as the acting U.S. Attorney for the District of Massachusetts in 1986-87. As Kevin Cullen has written, "Mueller was . . . in that position while Whitey Bulger was helping the FBI cart off his criminal competitors even as he buried bodies in shallow graves along the Neponset."[51]

What was the extent of Robert Mueller's knowledge or involvement in Boston's epic violence and federal corruption? As *The New American* observed in March of 2018, "To those who had been following the FBI-Winter Hill Gang activities for years, it was inconceivable that the corrupt relationships could have gone on for so long without the knowledge (and perhaps approval?) of higher-ups in the Bureau and the Department of Justice."[52]

What is further known, is what Robert Mueller ***did not do***: Robert Mueller did nothing to indict, prosecute or convict the homicidal Whitey Bulger or his deputies. Robert Mueller did nothing to indict, prosecute or convict the crooked and murderous federal agents who covered for, and assisted, Whitey Bulger's violent gang. Robert Mueller did nothing to get justice for the victims who were slain by the Boston gangsters and their allies in the Boston FBI— or for their families. Robert Mueller did nothing to get justice for Louis Greco, who was framed for murder with the help of the FBI and the FBI's solicitously protected informant, Joe Barbozo— and who died in prison for a murder he did not commit. And he did nothing to get justice for the children of Louis Greco, whose lives were destroyed by their father's false conviction.

What is also known is what Robert Mueller *did do*: He wrote multiple letters to parole and pardon boards opposing clemency for the four men the FBI helped convict for the murder of Teddy Deegan— including an innocent man— Louis Greco.

Robert Mueller was questioned in 2007 about the Boston FBI corruption that thrived while Mueller was an Assistant U.S. Attorney, and later an Acting U.S. Attorney. Kevin Cullen recorded Robert Mueller's response: "I think the public should recognize that what happened, happened years ago."[53]

Chapter 3

Pan Am 103

Mueller led the FBI's coverup of the December 21, 1988 bombing of Pan Am Flight 103.

Charles McKee was known for his gung ho attitude, patriotism and pursuit of excellence as an Army Officer with the Defense Intelligence Agency (DIA). And he was known for his size. At 6'5" and 270 pounds, McKee was known by his friends as "Tiny." Born in 1948, McKee graduated from Penn State in 1970 and joined the army that same year. He graduated first in his class in officers' training school at Fort Benning in Georgia; finished at the top of his class at least four times in highly specialized intelligence training; spoke fluent Arabic; and received "numerous military merit awards,"[54] including the Army Good Conduct Medal, National Defense Service Medal, and the Overseas Service Medal.

Roy Rowan, writing for *TIME Magazine*, described the Charles McKee known by his colleagues serving in intelligence in the Middle East:

> Major Charles Dennis McKee, called "Tiny" by his Army intelligence friends, was a burly giant and a superstar in just about every kind of commando training offered to American military personnel. He completed the rugged Airborne and Ranger schools, graduated first in his class from the Special Forces qualification course, and served with the Green Berets. In Beirut he was identified merely as a military

attaché assigned to the U.S. Defense Intelligence Agency (DIA). But his hulking physique didn't fit such a low-profile diplomatic post. Friends there remember him as a "walking arsenal" of guns and knives. His real assignment reportedly was to work with the CIA in reconnoitering the American hostages in Lebanon and then, if feasible, to lead a daring raid that would rescue them.

McKee's thick, 37-page Army dossier contains so many blacked-out words that it's hard to glean the danger he faced. Surviving the censor's ink was his title, "Team Chief." Under "Evaluation," it was written that he "performs constantly in the highest-stress environment with clear operational judgment and demeanor . . . Especially strong in accomplishing the mission with minimal guidance and supervision . . . Continues to perform one of the most hazardous and demanding jobs in the Army."[55]

Syracuse University maintains an archive on the victims of the Pan Am bombing, in part, to memorialize the 35 Syracuse students who were returning home for Christmas on December 21, 1988, from studying abroad in London and Florence— 35 students who died in the bombing. The Pan Am Archives of Syracuse include a tribute to Charles McKee: "Chuck was an extraordinary man who was described as having 'the right stuff.'"[56] McKee spent "the last ten years of an eighteen-year military career abroad."[57] His career— and his life— ended December 21, 1988, aboard Pan Am Flight 103. He was among 259 passengers that died when Pan Am 103 was blown apart in the skies over Lockerbie, Scotland.

Eleven residents of Lockerbie perished when the plane struck the ground in Scotland.

The January 31, 2001 verdict of three Scottish judges on the mid-air detonation of Pan Am Flight 103 seemed linear enough— at least to casual observers: Libyan intelligence officers Abdelbasat el-Megrahi and Lamin Khalifah Fhimah were convicted of planting a suitcase-embedded bomb on a Flight in Malta which ended up on Pan Am Flight 103 from London to America. Possibly, the prosecution theory went, the Pan Am bombing was retaliation by Libya, for American military strikes against Libyan fighter planes, ships and cities in the early and mid 1980s.

However, this apparition of justice has itself been exploded by the discoveries of researchers, intelligence professionals and victims' family members.

When Pan Am 103 exploded on December 21, 1988, it was carrying Charles McKee and his fellow intelligence officers. McKee and his colleagues were flying back home to America to blow the whistle on a CIA-assisted drug ring— that was trafficking heroin from the Middle East to American cities.

McKee, a Major in the Army, working for the Defense Intelligence Agency (DIA), and on temporary assignment with the CIA, had been sent to Lebanon to lead a team to rescue American hostages from Lebanon. However, while in the Mid-East, McKee and his peers had uncovered a rogue, terrorist-linked CIA unit, code-named COREA— after the Lebanese word for heroin, "kourah"— that was helping smuggle heroin into the United States. McKee and the DIA officers working with him were, according the Toronto Star, "outraged"[58] to find out that the CIA unit COREA was

19

involved in a drug operation that was smuggling heroin into American cities. To add fuel to their fire, COREA was working directly with a Syrian, international drug and arms dealer, Monzer al-Kassar, in trafficking heroin into the United States. Al-Kassar was working with COREA with what researcher Dean Henderson calls, "high-level CIA knowledge of his activities."[59]

In addition to their outrage over the CIA's involvement in trafficking drugs into America, and the CIA's ties to international criminals, McKee and his team were aghast that the CIA's dealings with Middle Eastern gangsters could endanger both McKee's team and the hostage rescue effort. As private security firm, Interfor, asserted, "The [McKee] Team was outraged, believing that its [hostage] rescue [operation] and their lives would be endangered by the double dealing."[60]

Interfor was the private security and investigative firm hired by Pan Am to investigate the bombing of Pan Am 103. Interfor's report on the Pan Am bombing was dismissed by many intelligence officials. Interfor was headed by former Israeli intelligent agent, Juval Aviv— and Israeli intelligence officials disputed that Aviv had ever worked with Israeli Intelligence. However, Interfor's conclusions constitute a searing indictment of the very officials that criticized Interfor's report, and Interfor's work undermined the credibility of some of the same Intelligence Officials who questioned Aviv's credentials. Moreover, *TIME Magazine*'s Roy Rowan confirmed that "a number of its findings appear well documented;"[61] and Interfor's report in fact dovetails with the conclusions of many independent investigations. Furthermore, as reported by Lisa Pease, Interfor had done work for the IRS and other federal agencies, and "had . . .

been hired by the Secret Service to investigate potential threats against President Reagan."[62]

McKee and his team complained directly to CIA headquarters about COREA's dangerous and illicit conduct. The CIA did not respond. Incensed by the CIA's non-response, McKee and his team resolved to fly to America, confront the CIA about COREA's operations— and expose COREA's conduct, if the CIA did not act decisively to rein them in.

On December 21, 1988, McKee and his team were flying back to America to confront the CIA about COREA's illicit, drug-smuggling operations.

Syrian Monzer al-Kassar, who was in his early 30s in 1988, was an arms dealer and drug trafficker. Al-Kassar was brother-in-law to Syria's intelligence chief, and his wife was related to Syrian President Hafez Assad.[63] A former spy for the DIA and DEA, had reportedly uncovered, through informants, that "al-Kassar and the Syrian President's brother Rifaat Assad were taking over drug production in Lebanon's Bekaa Valley, under protection of the Syrian army."[64] The drug ring run by al-Kassar was shipping heroin into American cities in the 1980s.

Following the bombing, Pan Am hired Interfor to find out who blew up the plane. According to the Interfor report, a CIA team in West Germany turned to al-Kassar to help secure the release of hostages held in the Mid East.[65] As the Interfor report further documented, in return for al-Kassar's cooperation in the release of hostages, COREA, a super-secret CIA cell in western Germany, protected al-Kassar's Middle Eastern heroin trafficking operation, which moved drugs through Pan Am's baggage handling section in

Frankfurt, through London, to America.[66]   At the same time, al-Kassar's drug operation was purportedly being used by the DEA, to track heroin shipments to Detroit, Los Angeles and Houston, and catch American drug dealers. During the same time frame that al-Kassar was working with the CIA and DEA and shipping heroin into America, he was also "part of the covert network run by [Ollie] North" and al-Kassar was given money by North's team to purchase small arms for the Contras.[67]

Thus, in the time period leading up to the destruction of Pan Am 103, al-Kassar was part of a super secret, drug-dealing CIA cell, COREA; he was working with the DEA, supposedly to catch American drug dealers; and he was purchasing weapons for Ollie North's covert team.

Al-Kassar's drug operation established a CIA-protected air route, which included a well-worn airport path, and a well-rehearsed team of drug smugglers, doubling as baggage handlers. According to the Interfor Report, baggage handlers at Pan Am's Frankfurt facilities, who were working with al-Kassar, would swap suitcases containing ordinary luggage with suitcases stuffed with drugs.[68]

In 1988, Ahmed Jibril was the boss of the Popular Front for the Liberation of Palestine-General Command (PFLP-G.C.) As Roy Rowan of *TIME Magazine* noted in June of 2001, "Almost immediately after the Pan Am bombing . . . the prime suspect was . . . Jibril."[69] Over 10 years later— after a decade of investigations, official and independent— Researcher Erick Anderson, pinpointed Jibril as "the man who masterminded and orchestrated the bombing of Flight 103."[70] The PBS program *Frontline* reached the same conclusion in November 1998.[71]

22

Two years before the Pan Am bombing, in a February 1986 press conference, Jibril had publicly vowed, "There will be no safety for any traveler on an Israeli or U.S. airliner."[72] Professor Ludwig de Braeckeleer, is a prolific chronicler of the Pan Am Investigation. Professor de Braeckeleer uncovered a DIA document that directly states that Jibril, of the PFLP-G.C., conducted the bombing: "In December 1988, Jibril conducted his first major international terrorist act since 1969, the bombing of Pan Am 103."[73]

De Braeckeleer has described the interaction between Iran and Jibril in the downing of Flight 103, the transaction in which Iran hired Jibril to bomb an American airliner, Iran's payments to Jibril for the crime— and Jibril's boast of committing the crime. According to de Braeckeleer, "US Intelligence agencies know that, a couple of days after the [July 3, 1988] downing of the [Iranian Airbus by the U.S.S. Vincennes], Ahmed Jibril contacted [Iranian Charge d'Affaires] Hussein Niknam"[74] to offer to conduct a revenge attack against the United States for pay. As de Braeckeleer further documents, "A DIA memo asserts that 'the operation was contracted to Jibril for [an advance payment of] $1 million.' The remainder was to be paid after successful completion of the mission."[75]

Intelligence officers not only intercepted Jibril's offer to Iran to bomb a U.S. airliner for pay, and the $1 million down payment from Iran to Jibril. They also intercepted the post-bombing congratulations from Iran to Jibril for the attack. Intelligence officers further listened in on the post-bombing request that the payment of the $10 million balance owed for the attack, be made to the terrorists, PFLP-G.C., for perpetrating the attack.

Thus, "On December 23, 1988, just two days after the downing of Pan Am 103, Israeli intelligence intercepted a phone call from Mohtashemi-Pur, [of] the [Iranian] Interior Ministry in Teheran, to [Iranian Charge d'Affaires] Hussein Niknam."[76] In this telephonic conversation, Mohtashemi-Pur congratulated Niknam for the "successful operation,"[77] and Mohtashemi-Pur directed Niknam to pay PFLP-G.C. the $10 million balance owed in payment for the bombing. A National Security Agency (NSA) report from 1991 similarly records that "[Iranian Official] Mohtashemi . . . was the one who paid the same amount [$10 million] to bomb Pan Am flight 103 in retaliation for the US shoot-down of the Iranian airbus."[78] As de Braeckeleer has documented, bank records confirm that Iran paid Jibril's group $10 million as the payment of the balance owed for the terrorist act. "The transaction— $10 million— is evidenced by a credit to a bank in Lausanne, Switzerland, and . . . the payment was moved from there to another PFLP-G.C. account at the Banque Nationale de Paris, and thence to the Hungarian development bank."[79]

De Braeckeleer states that in 2008, former Iranian President Abolhassan Bani-Sadr admitted "in the aftermath of the Lockerbie tragedy [that] Mohtashemi-Pur had claimed that he had personally ordered the bombing of Pan Am."[80] Further, after the "bombing of the Pan Am 103, Jibril held a champagne party during which he proudly declared: 'The Americans will never found out how I did it.'"[81] In a May 1989 meeting in Teheran, "Jibril proudly acknowledged to leaders of various Middle East Terrorism organizations that his group was responsible for the bombing of Pan Am 103."[82]

In 2001, *TIME Magazine* concurred that Iran paid Jibril and the PFLP-G.C. for bombing Pan Am 103, observing that Jibril's "banker for the attack on the Pan Am plane appeared to be Iran. U.S. intelligence agents even traced a wire transfer of several million dollars to a bank account in Vienna belonging to the PFLP-G.C."[83] Iran's motive was equally as obvious as their sponsorship: revenge for the mistaken shooting down of an Iranian airbus by the U.S.S. Vincennes in July 1988.

The evidence not only connects Palestinian militant, Ahmed Jibril, and the terrorist cell he led, PFLP-G.C., to the bombing. The evidence also connects Jibril to the CIA's international drug trafficking asset, Syrian, Monzer al-Kassar. By the fall of 1988, al-Kassar's drug operation had been noticed by PFLP-G.C. leader, Jibril. As reported by *TIME Magazine*, and according to Mossad, Jibril dined with al-Kassar, at a Paris restaurant. At that time, Jibril obtained al-Kassar's agreement, albeit reluctant, to assist in "planting a bomb aboard an as yet unselected American transatlantic jet."[84] Jibril determined to use al-Kassar's already established airport drug route, and luggage switching operation, to get a bomb on board an American plane.

"Two months [before the bombing], West German police [BKA] had arrested 16 members of [Jibril's] terrorist organization [PFLP-G.C.]."[85] Furthermore, when the BKA made the raids on Jibril's cell, they found "a plastic bomb concealed in a Toshiba cassette player, similar to the one that [later] blew up Flight 103."[86] Further, "BKA confiscated bombs [from PFLP-G.C.] made with the Czech explosive Serntex and hidden inside audio equipment, much like the one that destroyed Flight 103."[87]

At the time of the raids, two months before the Pan Am bombing, Jibril's assistant, Haffez Dalkamoni, was arrested in Frankfurt with known Jordanian bomb maker, Marwen Khreesat. Khreesat was reportedly an American intelligence asset.[88] Khreesat was curiously released. Jibril's right hand man, Dalkamoni, reportedly admitted that Khreesat-made bombs were at large elsewhere. U.S. intelligence officials later confirmed that members of Jibril's group "had been monitoring Pan Am's facilities at Frankfurt airport."[89]

In November, 1988, it apparently became expedient for Jibril to procure bomb components, possibly because the West German Police [BKA] had recently raided Jibril's PFLP-G.C. hiding places in Germany and seized the PFLP's bomb materials. According to the private investigative Report by Interfor, CIA asset, al-Kassar, helped transport bomb components from a Syrian living in Bulgaria, to Jibril's cell in West Germany. Several days before December 21, 1988, Jibril finalized the decision to target a Pan Am flight.

U.S. Government agencies, the CIA and the German police received multiple warnings about the impending disaster. Sixteen days before the bombing, on December 5, 1988, the FAA issued a security bulletin. This security alert recited that a man with an Arabic accent had called the U.S. Embassy in Helsinki, Finland, on that same date— December 5, 1988— and warned that a Pan Am Flight from Frankfurt to the United States would be blown up within the coming two weeks. The State Department sent the bulletin to dozens of embassies, and the FAA sent it to all U.S. airlines, including Pan Am. Within weeks before the bombing, "West German police and the CIA received a tip from Israeli intelligence about a possible terrorist attack against a U.S. carrier."[90] Researcher Erick Anderson summarizes, based on the Interfor Report, that "The CIA asked BKA [German police] to tighten security on all U.S. airlines *except* Pan Am . . . ."[91]

Al-Kassar had developed the airport drug smuggling route that was apparently used to get the bomb through baggage handling, and on board Pan Am 103. And Al-Kassar had reportedly delivered bomb components, for the bomb. Quixotically, Al-Kassar also tipped off the CIA about the Pan Am bombing for which he (al-Kassar) had developed the airport drug smuggling route used to get the bomb aboard, and for which he had reportedly delivered bomb components. Thus, according to Researcher Erick Anderson, on or about December 18, 1988, al-Kassar and his cell "warned [the German police] BKA the attack would be on Pan Am's regular Frankfurt-London-New York flight within the next 3 days."[92]   Perhaps, al-Kassar was playing both sides of the fence.   Maybe he had compunction about the impending, massive loss of innocent life.   Too, the CIA might have misled him (al-Kassar) into believing that he was working a sting to nail Jibril for an attempted terrorist attack, and that the CIA would stop the bombing in the nick of time— before apprehending Jibril.

The Interfor Report indicates, moreover, that a few days before the bombing, "a BKA undercover officer reported Pan Am would be the target of a bomb attempt within the next two or three days"[93]— a warning that BKA relayed to the CIA's COREA cell.

David Lovejoy was an alleged double agent with the CIA, who had previously struck weapons deals favorable to the Iranians. According to a report in *TIME Magazine*, based on a story appearing in the Arabic newspaper *Al-Dunstur* on May 22, 1989, CIA Agent Lovejoy informed the Iranian Embassy in Beirut about the travel plans of McKee's team, to fly back to America.   Further, Pan Am lawyer James Shaughnessy averred in an affidavit filed with federal district court in New York, that "in November and December 1988 the U.S. government intercepted a series of telephone calls from [CIA Agent] Lovejoy to the Iranian charge d'affaires in Beirut advising him of [McKee's] team's movements."[94] Moreover, "Lovejoy's last call came on Dec. 20, allegedly informing the Iranians that [McKee's] team would be on Pan Am Flight 103 the following day."[95]

Interfor reported that 24 hours before the December 21, 1988 Pan Am flight, "an undercover agent from . . . Mossad report[ed] to BKA about a plan to place a bomb on that very Pan Am flight."[96] BKA informed COREA of the warning from Israeli intelligence, that there was a plot to bomb Pan Am 103. COREA reported the warning to its CIA Control. CIA Control reportedly gave no guidance.

German Police [BKA] surveillance agents, were alerted to the bomb warnings. "The BKA surveillance agent watching the Pan Am flight load December 21st noticed that the 'drug' suitcase was different in make, shape, material and color"[97] from the customary drug shipments. "The agent, alert to the bomb warnings, reported to his [BKA] superiors that something was very wrong."[98] BKA headquarters informed the CIA Unit COREA about the alarming development of the suspicious luggage intended for Pan Am Flight 103.

Moreover, "Al-Kassar [had already] contacted the same CIA unit . . . to let them know that McKee and the five other agents were flying home that day."[99]

COREA told its CIA Control that it was imminent that an apparent bomb was going to be loaded on Pan Am 103, on December 21, 1988. The CIA already knew that Charles McKee was going to be on board Pan Am 103 on December 21, 1988. On the very date McKee's team was flying home on Pan Am 103, and in the wake of the multiple warnings of an airliner bombing, COREA advised its CIA Control that a suspicious piece of luggage was being loaded onto Pan Am 103.

Thus, COREA informed its CIA Control, that there was a plan to bomb the Pan Am 103 Flight that Charles McKee and his team were scheduled to take from London to America. CIA Control directed that Flight 103— with its living cargo of Major McKee's team, and its ominous, explosive freight— not be stopped.

Interfor uncovered the CIA Control's instruction to the COREA CIA unit on the ground in Germany on December 21, 1988, concerning Pan Am Flight 103. In what was perhaps Interfor's most explosive finding, Interfor documented CIA Control's instruction to the COREA CIA unit about Pan Am Flight 103 on December 21, 1988. That instruction? "[CIA] Control replied: don't worry about it, don't stop it, let it go."[100]

A drug smuggling air route and luggage-switching operation that functioned in airports in Frankfurt and London had been established by Monzer al-Kassar, the CIA asset, and Syrian arms and drug dealer. As Interfor reports corroborated, this smuggling route and operation in Frankfurt and London, had been used by Ahmed Jibril and his group PFLP-G.C., the Syrian-based terrorist cell hired by Iran to bomb an American flight. In short, al-Kassar developed the airport smuggling route for drugs; Jibril used it for the bombing.

Post-bombing investigation further confirmed that this mass murder in mid-air was committed using the Frankfurt to London drug smuggling route and operation that was developed by al-Kassar and used by Jibril. In January 1990,

Interfor, the private security firm hired by Pan Am to investigate the bombing; Pan Am's legal team; and a former U.S. Army polygrapher, conducted lie detector tests on the only two Pan Am baggage handlers in Frankfurt who were in a position to switch suitcases. "As the polygraphist later testified before a federal grand jury in Washington,"[101] the first baggage handler, administered the test three times, "was not truthful when he said he did not switch the suitcases."[102] As the polygraphist further testified before the same grand jury, the second baggage handler, administered the test two times, was not truthful "when he stated he did not see the suitcase being switched, and when he stated that he did not know what was in the switched suitcase."[103]

As for the London part of the trip, it was revealed in 2009, that at some time during the 2-hour period before 12:35 a.m. on December 21, 1988, the padlock on the area leading to Pan Am's baggage handling area at London's Heathrow Airport was broken. Pan Am's baggage area in London had been broken into— 17 hours before the Pan Am Flight 103 took off from London. Post bombing revelations are arguably consistent with switching a suitcase full of drugs with ordinary luggage in Frankfurt, and the placement of a bomb in the baggage loading area in London.

William Taylor, the English counsel that represented the Libyan defendants, claimed the bomb could have been planted during the break-in at Heathrow. As Dean Henderson summarizes, *Frontline* came to a similar conclusion:

> A PBS *Frontline* investigation found evidence that the bomb was actually planted while Flight 103 stopped over at London's Heathrow Airport. A suitcase belonging to CIA agent Matthew Gannon, one of the five others on

Colonel McKee's team, was switched with [the] bag at Heathrow. *Frontline* believes Gannon's suitcase may have contained information linking the Damascus-based COREA CIA cell with al-Kassar's drug ring, so the suitcase was stolen and one containing the bomb was substituted for it.[104]

Following the bombing, CIA Agents descended on Scotland in droves to seize, alter and destroy evidence. "[L]ocals were perturbed by the immediate presence of large numbers of Americans who showed up in Lockerbie within a couple of hours of the downing of the plane." Airborne federal agents trained rifles on the Lockerbie locals. As reported by Gareth Peirce, in "The Framing of al-Megrahi," for the *London Review of Books,*

> Extraordinarily, however, distinct from the Dumfries and Galloway police [in Scotland], scores of men, some wearing no insignia, some the insignia of the FBI and Pan Am (it was noted at the time that many of these men were clearly not Pan Am staff), invaded the area. Lockerbie residents reported seeing unmarked helicopters hovering overhead, carrying men with rifles whose telescopic sights were pointing directly at them.[105]

The Agents' actions, in keeping the natives at bay, reflected a frantic concern that civilians might find evidence in the wreckage that could incriminate covert operations gone corrupt, before federal agents got to it. Indeed, CIA Agents told Scottish officials they were looking for "something of great importance, but would not specify what it was. They told the Scottish officials they'd know it when they found it."[106] In *Lockerbie: The Real Story*, author David Johnston depicted the actions of CIA agents in landing in Lockerbie by helicopter, searching for McKee's brief case. Johnston documented that a sheep farmer was kept off part of his property, while CIA agents retrieved the baggage of Charles McKee.

The CIA violated basic rules of Crime Scene investigation, by removing McKee's suitcase to an unknown location, without documenting its recovery, location or removal with the local Scottish Investigators on the ground. As Johnston wrote, "Having found part of their quarry, the CIA had no intention of following the exacting rules of evidence employed by the Scottish police. They took the suitcase and its contents into the chopper and flew with it to an unknown destination."[107] In *Lockerbie: Flight from Justice,* author, Paul Foot, verified that the "suitcase belonging to Major Charles McKee . . . had been mysteriously carried away from the piles of wreckage left by the crash . . . ."[108] The CIA returned McKee's suitcase with the same disregard for procedures of evidentiary preservation— and with a false cover story.

Thus, several days later, Johnston reports, the CIA returned the suitcase to the place it was discovered, where it was "found" by two British Transport officers "who in their ignorance were quite happy to sign statements about the [suit]case's discovery."[109]

However, when the suitcase was returned by the CIA, the suitcase had a rectangular opening cut in its shell, which the CIA had presumably used to empty the suitcase of its contents. According to author Paul Foot, McKee's suitcase "had a large hole cut into it before it was returned to the investigators. The specific intention of cutting the hole, it was agreed, was to inspect the contents of the suitcase long before its evidential value could be established."[110]   In short, federal agents removed the contents of McKee's suitcase.

What was in the suitcase that the federal agents were desperate to hide or destroy? Was it McKee's records about the CIA's involvement in the drug smuggling ring of al-Kassar, which was importing heroin into the United States?

The CIA not only purloined the contents of the suitcase. Someone in the investigation also attempted to fabricate a lie about what had been in McKee's briefcase. Federal agents and the Prosecution team attempted to mislead the Scottish Court that heard the case, into believing that the contents of McKee's suitcase were not sensitive intelligence about the CIA's drug network and ties to Middle Eastern terrorists— but clothing.

However, as clarified by forensic expert, Dr. Thomas Hayes, at the trial conducted in 2000, the clothing tendered to him and represented as being taken from McKee's suitcase, unlike the suitcase from which the clothing was "*supposedly* taken[,] showed little evidence of explosives (sic) involvement."[111]   Dr. Hayes acknowledged at trial that he chose the word "supposedly"[112] with care, in reciting that clothing proffered in evidence was "supposedly" taken from McKee's suitcase. He further clarified that it was "one interpretation,"[113] that the clothing that had been represented to be the contents of McKee's was not in fact taken from McKee's suitcase. Dr. Hayes also assented that it was reasonable— "an inference that could be drawn"[114]— that someone had interfered with the suitcase following the disaster and before it was made available to him for forensic examination.

In sum, the CIA seized Major McKee's suitcase; illegally removed it from the Crash Scene; cut a hole in it; stole its presumably sensitive, interior contents, that potentially implicated the CIA in an international drug ring; returned it without recording the fact that it had been removed and returned; returned it without truthfully documenting chain of custody; fabricated the false story that it was recovered by local constabularies; and presented the false story that the contents of McKee's suitcase was not vital evidence of the CIA's drug trafficking and links to terrorists— but clothing.

The federal effort to cover up evidence relating to Charles McKee did not stop there. After McKee's death, "FBI agents visited [McKee's] mother to ask if her son had left any packages with her. Agents said some of her son's belongings found in his luggage could not be returned and would be destroyed in the interests of national security."[115]

Also found at the Scene was contraband which prospectively confirmed the later reports of Interfor and others, that al-Kassar's drug ring was using Pan Am flights to traffic heroin into America. As Lisa Pease put it, "[A]ccording to a few key witnesses, something else was found [at the Scene]. Drugs. Heroin, to be exact."[116]

Federal authorities, the CIA and the national law enforcement of other countries, participated in stonewalling any independent investigation of the bombing, and destroyed— or "lost"— critical evidence. Although Pan Am's legal counsel, James Shaughnessy, previously subpoenaed "the FBI, CIA, DEA and four other government agencies for all documents pertaining to both the bombing of Flight 103 and the [DEA] narcotics sting operation [with al-Kassar], he has been repeatedly rebuffed by the Justice Department for reasons of national security."[117]

Some of the most critical evidence in the investigation was destroyed, has disappeared— or was "lost". That classification— "lost"— is not limited to the contents of Major McKee's briefcase. That description further encompasses the Investigative Report of the break-in at London's Heathrow some 17 hours before the Flight— lost. That description likewise includes the BKA's videotape of the handling of baggage at Pan Am's Frankfurt airport the day of the bombing, the existence of which videotape was discovered by Interfor. That videotape? Also lost. Though Interfor claims that the CIA also had a copy of that videotape, the CIA has never made that videotape public, or provided it to the courts.

The principal involvement of the Iranians and Syrians in the bombing is established by the evidence and confirmed by intelligence experts. DIA documents, Israeli intelligence, and the sleuthing of independent investigators have all confirmed that Iran *paid for* the attack, and the Syrian-based Jibril and his PFLP-G.C. *committed* the attack. Robert Baer, an ex-CIA Agent who worked on the original investigation into the Pan Am bombing, "has claimed that 'to a man' the CIA believes Iran was responsible for the terrorist attack."[118] According to the *London Daily Telegraph*, Baer claimed that the Syrian-based terrorist group, the PFLP-G.C., "built the bomb and put it on board Pan Am Flight 103."[119] Baer further stated that "his views were 'not controversial' in intelligence circles, where Iran's involvement was accepted."[120] Baer also noted that "the CIA had 'grade A' intelligence that two PFLP-G.C. members suspected of involvement in Lockerbie, [Jibril's henchmen] Mohammed Abu Talib and [Jibril's Lieutenant] Hafez (sic) Dalkamoni were named on an honour roll in Iran for a 'great service' they had performed for the country."[121]

Multiple intelligence sources confirmed that Iran contracted with Jibril to take out an American Flight; before the Flight was bombed, Iran paid Jibril a down payment of $1 million; after the bombing, Iran paid Jibril $10 million for the balance owed for executing the bombing— and Jibril bragged of committing the crime.

Evidence of Iranian and Syrian involvement is abundant. The CIA's fingerprints on the crime, likewise cannot be credibly denied. The CIA seized, and presumably destroyed, the contents of Charles McKee's suitcase, which would have implicated the CIA cell COREA in a Middle Eastern smuggling ring, that was helping transport heroin into American cities. Monzer al-Kassar, who developed the drug air route and smuggling operation that was apparently used to place a bomb on board Pan Am 103, was a CIA asset. That same drug air route and smuggling operation, used to commit the bombing, was protected by the CIA. Al-Kassar who, according to Interfor, delivered bomb components to Jibril's terrorist cell in Germany, was— again— a CIA asset. Marwan Khreesat, who was building bombs for Jibril and the PFLP-G.C. before the Pan Am bombing— like the one used to destroy Pan Am 103— was arrested with Jibril's Lieutenant, Haffez Dalkamoni, approximately six weeks before the crime. According to some researchers, Khreesat was a CIA asset.[122] The CIA ignored repeated warnings pointing to a terrorist-planned bombing of Flight 103. In the time frame leading up to the bombing, and in the wake of multiple warnings about an airliner bombing, the CIA asked the German police to tighten security on all U.S. airlines— except Pan Am. A CIA Agent, David Lovejoy, apparently tipped off Iranian officials that McKee and his team intended to board the Pan Am Flight. The CIA, according to Interfor, gave the final go ahead to the mass execution. According to

Interfor's Report, "(CIA) Control replied: don't worry about it, don't stop it, let it go."

As Roy Rowan of *TIME Magazine* reported,

> Victor Marchetti, former executive assistant to the CIA's deputy director and co-author of *The CIA and the Cult of Intelligence,* believes that the presence of the [McKee] team on Flight 103 is a clue that should not be ignored. His contacts at Langley agree. "It's like the loose thread of a sweater," he says. "Pull on it, and the whole thing may unravel."[123]

Gene Wheaton, a retired U.S. military-intelligence officer with 17 years experience, serving as an Investigator for the families of crash victims, has come to a similar conclusion: "Retired Air Force investigator Gene Wheaton thinks [Major] Charles McKee and the five other honorable CIA agents were the bomber's primary targets."[124] As Wheaton has stated, "A couple of my old black ops buddies in the Pentagon believe the Pan Am bombers were gunning for McKee's hostage-rescue team . . . ."[125] Kevin Ryan has noted,

> With the Pan Am 103 case, Mueller was covering up facts related to some of the victims of the bombing—a group of U.S. intelligence specialists led by Major Charles McKee of the Defense Intelligence Agency. McKee had gone to Beirut to find and rescue hostages and, while there, learned about CIA involvement in a drug smuggling operation run through an agency project called COREA. As *TIME magazine*

reported, the likely explanation for the bombing, supported by independent intelligence experts, was that U.S. operatives "targeted Flight 103 in order to kill the hostage-rescue team." This would prevent disclosure of what McKee's team had learned. That theory was also supported by the fact that the CIA showed up immediately at the scene of the crash, took McKee's briefcase, and returned it empty.[126]

As Charles Norrie, author of *A Tale of Three Atrocities* observed: "The explanation came to me very quickly indeed. Poor McKee was killed by his colleagues."[127]

Charles McKee's mother, Beulah McKee, had difficulty foreclosing the notion that Pan Am was targeted because her son was aboard. "The government's secrecy can't close off my mind,"[128] she told Roy Rowan of *TIME Magazine*. It was difficult, moreover, for her to get answers out of Susan Gannon. Susan Gannon is the widow of Matthew Gannon. Matthew Gannon was the rising CIA star who was part of Charles McKee's team, and who died with Charles McKee aboard Pan Am 103. Susan Gannon is also the daughter of Thomas Twetten, who in 1988 was head of the CIA's Near East Division. Susan Gannon herself worked for the CIA.

At least twice Mrs. McKee called Susan Gannon to try to get answers. The last time she called her, Susan Gannon, did not give Mrs. McKee information— but an admonition against talking too much. As Mrs. McKee told Roy Rowan, "The last time, I was accused of opening my mouth too much."[129] Finally, it's hard for Beulah McKee to accept the government cover story about Pan Am 103. "I know that's not what our President wants me to say,"[130] she told Roy

Rowan about the preferences of President George W. Bush. But "[f]or three years, I've had a feeling that if Chuck hadn't been on that plane, it wouldn't have been bombed."[131]

Iranian involvement in the Pan Am bombing was the intelligence community's firm conclusion. As ex-CIA Agent, Robert Baer, has proclaimed, there was unanimity among the rank and file of federal intelligence officers, that Iran was behind the bombing. As writer, Bill Blum, of *Consortiumnews.com*, observed, the Iranian-PLFP-G.C. Conspiracy "was the Original Official Version, delivered with Olympian rectitude by the U.S. government, guaranteed, sworn to, scout's honor, case closed . . . ."[132] Author David Johnston devoted a chapter of *Lockerbie: The Tragedy of Flight 103* "to the prevalent theory in the months following the attack, that the . . . (PFLP-GC) was responsible."[133]

Scottish journalist Magnus Linklater, similarly observed that

It is sometimes forgotten just how powerful the evidence was, in the first few months after Lockerbie, that pointed towards the involvement of the Palestinian-Syrian terror group the PFLP-GC, backed by Iran and linked closely to terror groups in Europe. . . . [W]e were strongly briefed by police and ministers to concentrate on this link, with revenge for an American rocket attack on an Iranian airliner as the motive.[134]

As Pease further notes,

[T]he *Sunday Times* of London reported in its front-page headline of March 26, 1989,

'Pan Am Bombers Identified.' The article stated that anonymous intelligence sources knew who was behind the bombing: 'the Popular Front for the Liberation of Palestine, General Command [PFLP-G.C.], led by Ahmed Jibril, a Damascus-based PLO renegade . . . .'[135]

As *TIME Magazine* reported, "Even Vincent Cannistraro, former head of the CIA's investigation of the bombing, told The New York Times [about subsequent efforts to blame the bombing on Libya] it was 'outrageous' to pin the whole thing on Libyan leader Muammar Gaddafi."[136]

And so, the guilt of Iran and the Syrian-based PFLP-G.C. was the accepted version— until the Investigation was precipitously re-routed. However, the investigation did not take a precipitous U-turn because of evidence, facts or analysis— but because of international politics. Iran and the Syrian-linked PFLP-G.C. were deemed the guilty parties until, as Bill Blum recounts, "the Gulf War came along in 1990 and the support of Iran and Syria were needed."[137] Thus, "in the fall of 1990 . . . President George H.W. Bush was scrambling to assemble a coalition to drive Iraqi troops out of Kuwait."[138] Moreover, the Bush I administration not only needed military allies in the Iraq War. The Bush administration also needed "Iranian and Syrian help, too, in freeing U.S. hostages then held by Islamic militant groups in Lebanon."[139] Finally, Pease observes, "[I]n 1990, spin-off investigations from the Iran-Contra scandal were underway with Iranian officials possessing possible information that could have incriminated President Bush as he was looking toward a tough reelection battle in 1992."[140] In the final analysis, Pease observes, "the Iranians held a number of cards that would have made them inconvenient targets of the Pan Am investigation."[141]

Libya, on the other hand, was a ready scapegoat. As London's *Daily Telegraph* reported on March 11, 2014, ex-CIA Agent Robert Baer indicated not only that there was universal consensus among rank and file CIA Agents that Iran was behind the attack— but that "Libya was made a convenient scapegoat for Lockerbie because it was a pariah state." As Peace has noted, "the Libyans were opposing Bush's Persian Gulf Intervention and had long ranked near the top of the list of America's favorite enemies. Laying the blame on the Libyans let a lot of influential people off the hook."[142]

Thus, "The direction of the case shifted dramatically in the fall of 1990 . . . ."[143] As Dean Henderson has reported, "Columnist Jack Anderson reported a telephone conversation between President Bush Sr. and British Prime Minister Margaret Thatcher after the crash in which both agreed that the investigation should be limited, so as not to harm the nations' intelligence communities."[144] Suddenly, stated Henderson, "Both the US and Britain . . . engaged in a coverup of the facts."

Thus, in the fall of 1991, out of the blue, "the U.S. Justice Department blamed the bombing on two Libyans, Abdel Basset Ali al-Megrahi and Lamen Khalifa Fhimah."[145] The Justice Department accused al-Megrahi and Fhimah of the crime over three years after the attack, even though they had not previously been connected to the crime by evidence, investigation or media reports. Suddenly, because of political expedience, al-Megrahi was "one of the Libyans made patsy for the bombing."[146]

The three-year investigation was conducted by the local Scottish Police— the Dumphries and Galloway

Constabulary— and the FBI. Ultimately, after the Department of Justice made its prosecutorial decision, indictments for murder were brought against Libyan Intelligence Officers Abdel Basset Ali al-Megrahi and Lamen Khalifa Fhimah on November 13, 1991.

Al-Megrahi and Lamen Khalifa Fhimah were tried in The Netherlands beginning May 3, 2000, before a panel of three Scottish Judges. The case brought by authorities was, as Kevin Ryan noted, "a flimsy story that accused a Libyan named Megrahi of coordinating placement of a suitcase bomb that allegedly traveled unaccompanied through several airports to find its way to the doomed flight."[147] Ryan called the charge against the Libyans an "unbelievable tale."[148]

The charges essentially asserted that al-Megrahi moved a bomb undetected from Malta to Frankfurt to London and through the London airport, through the security apparati at the Malta Airport, the Frankfurt Airport and the London Airport, and on to Pan Am 103, without accompanying or personally transporting the explosive; without an established network of on-the-take baggage handlers; without the operational assistance of a drug ring or terrorist cell; without the support of the CIA; without the tacit assistance of European police departments tasked to look the other way. Authorities effectively charged that al-Megrahi remotely controlled the transit of a bomb through three airports, through at least three airport security systems, without being present, without an established luggage smuggling and switching operation, without the help of terrorist cells, without the assistance of corrupt intelligence officers, without the support of corrupt law enforcement, without inside connections— without any help at all.

Frankfurt's Airport security alone, included "[s]ecurity officers using video cameras routinely keep[ing] watch over the area[,] [a]n intricate network of computerized conveyors, the most sophisticated baggage-transfer system in the world . . . ."[149] Further, "Every piece of luggage is logged minute by minute from one position to the next, so its journey through the airport is carefully monitored. The bags are then X-rayed by the airline before being put aboard a plane."[150] Concluded Rowan, "the U.S. government's charges against al-Megrahi and Fhimah don't explain how the bronze-colored Samsonite suitcase [carrying the bomb], dispatched via Air Malta, eluded Frankfurt's elaborate airport security system."[151]

The conviction of al-Megrahi was supposedly "nailed down"[152] by a printout from a German company that purportedly showed that a suitcase sent from Malta through Frankfurt was ultimately placed aboard Pan Am 103 in London. However, as *TIME Magazine* uncovered, an FBI memo documents that the "handwritten record kept"[153] by the baggage handler documents only that luggage was unloaded from the December 21, 1988 Air Malta Flight 180 from Malta to Frankfurt— without indicating "how much baggage was unloaded or where the luggage was sent."[154] Ultimately, "The FBI agent's report concludes, 'There remains the possibility that no luggage was transferred from Air Malta 180 to Pan Am 103.'"[155]

The prosecution's theory is further transected by the testimony of 20 officials who were in Malta on December 21, 1988,

including the airport security commander, the bomb-disposal engineer who inspected all the baggage, the general manager of ground operations, the head loader of [Air Malta] Flight 180 [the feeder flight for the Frankfurt flight to London] and the three check-in agents. Their records showed that no unaccompanied suitcases were put aboard the flight [from Malta to Frankfurt] . . . .[156]

As Rowan records, several officials were able to vouchsafe that "there was no bag that day [on the Malta to Frankfurt flight] destined for Pan Am 103."[157]

Moreover, more recent investigation reveals that the subject suitcase, later known to transport the bomb, was seen by a baggage handler on the bottom floor of the luggage transfer container at Heathrow at approximately 4:45 p.m.— about one hour before the flight from Malta through Frankfurt arrived. As noted by Author M.G. Kerr, this observation indicates that the subject suitcase-embedded bomb did not arrive from Frankfurt— or Malta. Simply stated, the suitcase-embedded bomb was already in London's Heathrow, before the Flight from Frankfurt arrived in London. According to this evidence, the bomb did not swim its way unaccompanied, upstream, from Malta to Frankfurt to London.

It was the Prosecution's theory that al-Megrahi remote-controlled a suitcase-embedded bomb through the security system of three airports without the assistance of a network of in-airport operatives, and without inside help. The Prosecution's theory was not only highly attenuated— but repudiated by the totality of the evidence. The Prosecution could therefore not base its case on the spurious theory of an unaccompanied, "remote-controlled" suitcase embedded bomb inexplicably guiding itself through three international airports. The Prosecution had to manufacture some plausible basis for the indictment and arrest of al-Megrahi. Thus, instead of focusing on the alleged airport-path of the bomb, "the indictment zeroes in on two tiny pieces of forensic evidence— a fingernail-size fragment of green plastic from a Swiss digital timer, and a charred piece of shirt."[158] Under rigorous analysis— and post-trial revelations— these two pieces of forensic evidence were demonstrated to be as spurious as the theory of a remote-controlled suitcase.

The Prosecution alleged that the Pan Am bomb was wrapped in a shirt purchased in Malta— and that al-Megrahi purchased that shirt. The statements, testimony and putative identifications by the Maltese shop owner, Tony Gauci, that supposedly identified al-Megrahi as the purchaser of the shirt, were spectacular in their inconsistencies. As Gareth Peirce, wrote for the *London Review of Books*, Gauci described the purchaser as 6'0"— Megrahi was 5'8". Gauci described the purchaser as 50 years old— Megrahi was 37. Gauci identified people other than Megrahi as the purchaser. Thus, Gauci identified the purchaser as a CIA Agent; and Gauci asserted that the purchaser was "like the man [pictured] in the *Sunday Times*"[159]— Jibril's PFLP-G.C. henchman, Abu Talb.

Megrahi was in Malta on December 7, 1988. Yet Gauci testified that the purchase of the shirt occurred before the Christmas lights were turned on for the year— and Christmas lights were turned on for the year on December 6, 1988. In short, al-Megrahi was in the store on December 7; according to Gauci, the purchase was made before December 6. Gauci asserted that Megrahi had been in his store before the purchase, at the time of the purchase, after the purchase— and also averred that Megrahi "had been there only once."[160]

Many terms could be used to describe Gauci's attestation that Megrahi was the shirt purchaser— "positive identification" is not one of them. Thus, as Peirce reports,

Gauci asserted Megrahi was "similar [to the purchaser] but not identical;"[161] Megrahi was "perhaps like him [the purchaser], but not fully like him."[162] Even the Scottish Court that convicted Megrahi, had to acknowledge the flawed nature of Gauci's identification, tactfully admitting "a substantial discrepancy."[163]

However, Gauci was reportedly interviewed 23 times; according to Peirce, Gauci received payment for his testimony; and he "apparently now lives in Australia, supported by millions of US dollars."[164] After the intensive "preparation" for his testimony; in anticipation of the monetary reward; and despite testimonial inconsistencies about the size of the man that purchased the shirt, the age of the man, the identity of the man, the appearance of the man, the date of the purchase, how many times the man had been there, when the man had been there— Gauci arguably did what he was expected to do: identify al-Megrahi in court as the purchaser of the fateful shirt. Which he did: "He resembles him a lot."[165]

The second element of material evidence, the bomb components, ended up being no less delusory than the first. In the first instance, bombs were seized in Frankfurt, two months before the bombing, in a raid on the PFLP-G.C.— the Iranian and Syrian sponsored, Palestinian terrorists led by Ahmed Jibril. The seized bombs included a bomb in a Toshiba cassette radio wired to a barometric timer switch— like the bomb used to blow up Pan Am 103. Moreover, as Peirce reports, when the debris of the crash were put together by the Dumphries and Galloway police, "fragments of a Toshiba cassette radio were found"[166]— fragments from the same type of electronic device that were known to be included in the bombs possessed by Jibril's terrorist cell.

46

As Peirce notes, the Toshiba cassette bombs seized from Jibril, were designed to detonate approximately 37 to 38 minutes after takeoff: it takes a plane 7 or 8 minutes to get to sufficient altitude for barometric pressure to drop, and activate a barometric timer set to go off and trigger the explosive 30 minutes later. As Peirce states, "It was precisely 38 minutes after Pan Am Flight 103 took off from Heathrow on 21 December 1988 that it exploded over Lockerbie . . . ."[167]

As Peirce further reports, Jibril's right hand man, Haffez Dalkamoni, was arrested in Frankfurt, in October 1988, with notorious bomb-maker, and suspected CIA asset, Marwan Khreesat, "as they visited electrical shops in the city."[168] Found in Dalkamoni's car at the time of his arrest, some 2 months before the Pan Am bombing, was a "Toshiba cassette recorder, . . . a simple time delay switch, and a barometric switch"[169]— bomb components with the same design as the bomb that brought down Pan Am 103. States Peirce,

> Dalkamoni admitted he had [previously] supervised Khreesat when he built bombs into a Toshiba radio cassette player, two radio tuners and a TV monitor. Dalkamoni admitted that other bombs made by Khreesat were at large— including a bomb built into a second Toshiba player, with similar pressure switches to the bomb used to down Pan Am 103.[170]

In short, two months before the disaster, the components of a bomb, including a Toshiba Cassette Player, like the components of the bomb that brought down Pan Am 103, were found in the vehicle of Jibril's soldier, Dalkamoni. A second bomb, built into a Toshiba cassette player, and thus

47

consistent with the bomb used to destroy Pan Am 103, had been built by the PFLP-G.C.'s criminal associate, Khreesat, and was at large. Dalkamoni admitted that he had supervised Khreesat in the construction of bombs, including one built into a Toshiba cassette player— like the bomb used to fell Pan Am 103.

Independent researchers believe, and the evidence indicates, that someone in the Pan Am Prosecution destroyed, fabricated and planted evidence to convict the Libyan, al-Megrahi. FBI Task Force Chief Richard Marquise stated that, without the fragment of a bomb timer introduced at trial, "It would be a very difficult case to prove . . . . I don't think we would ever [have] had an indictment."[171] Thomas Thurman, the FBI's lead Forensic Investigator stated that the timer fragment was the "only real piece of evidence against Libya."[172]

The fragment of a circuit board, that was part of an electronic timer, which was in turn part of the bomb that blew up Pan Am 103, was found at the Scene. The FBI essentially contended that this timer fragment proved the guilt of Libyans— and steered the case away from Jibril, the PFLP-G.C., Syria and Iran. The type of circuit board, a fragment of which was found at the Scene, was a *brown 8-ply circuit board.* The Swiss bomb-maker, Mebo, did not supply timers with brown 8-ply circuit boards to the Libyans. The type of timer sold by Mebo to Libyans, on the other hand, had a *green 9-ply circuit board.* In short, the circuit board fragment found at the Scene did *not* come from the type of circuit board *furnished to* the Libyans, nor did it come from the type of circuit board *used by* the Libyans.

Someone in the investigation apparently switched a fragment from a *green 9-ply circuit board* typically used by

Libyans, for the fragment of a brown *8-ply circuit board* that was actually found at the Scene. Thus, the Prosecution arguably attempted to switch a *green 9-ply circuit board* fragment of the type of circuit board used by Libya, *for* the *brown 8-ply circuit board* fragment that was discovered at the Scene and that was not of the type of circuit board used by Libya. They removed actual evidence and replaced it with planted evidence— in an evidence "swap."

According to outside observers, the switch or planting of evidence, was done to falsely misdirect the investigation towards Libya— and away from the Syrian-connected and Iranian-sponsored PFLP-G.C.

The transfer and planting of evidence was exposed by several developments in the proceedings. After trial, in July 2007, an employee of Swiss Bomb Manufacturer, Mebo, admitted by affidavit, that he stole a *green 9-ply circuit board* of the type used by Libya, and gave it to one of the official investigators in the case. Obtaining a *green 9-ply circuit board* of the type used by Libya, allowed Investigators to swap a Libyan-favored *green 9-ply circuit board* fragment, for the *brown 8-ply circuit board* fragment that was actually found at the Scene, and that was not of the type used by the Libyans.

Moreover, as Gareth Peirce has noted, the lead British Investigator, Thomas Hayes, kept a thorough, meticulous, detailed record of physical evidence recovered in the Scene Investigation.[173] It was his practice, in Crime Scene Investigations, to draw on a grid the location of items of physical evidence found at a Crime Scene; and assign the piece of physical evidence an exhibit number that denoted the sequence of its recovery. However, with respect to this critical timer fragment— one of the most critical pieces of evidence in the case— Hayes abandoned his own rigorous protocol: Hayes didn't log it on a grid; he didn't give it an exhibit number that corresponded with the sequence of its recovery; and the original page of his notes that documented the recovery of the timer fragment was apparently lost— or discarded.

Edwin Bollier, the owner of the Swiss Manufacturer, Mebo, was asked by police *before trial* to identify the fragment of a brown 8-ply circuit board that was found at the Scene. The fragment actually found at the Scene came from a brown 8-ply circuit board, which Bollier's Company, Mebo, never supplied to Libya. However, at trial in 2000, the Prosecution tried to get Bollier to imply that that the circuit board fragment found at the Scene was the same type that was sold to, and used, by the Libyans— that it came from a *green 9-ply circuit board*— when in fact the *brown 8-ply circuit board* fragment that was actually found at the Scene, did not come from the type of circuit board that was supplied to the Libyans. In effect, the Prosecution attempted to use Bollier's testimony to falsely portray that a fragment from a green *9-ply circuit board*, of the type sold to Libya, had been found at the Scene, when in fact, a fragment from a *brown 8-ply circuit board* which Bollier's company never sold to Libya, was found at the Scene.

The Lockerbie trial was held in 2000. Bollier revealed to BBC in 2007, that when Bollier visited the FBI headquarters in early 1991, he was offered a bribe of $4 million, and a new identity in the United States, if he would falsely testify in court that the circuit board fragment actually found at the Scene, came from the type of timer his company routinely sold to Libya.

Found at the Scene were traces of high power explosives RDX and PETN. In a post-trial documentary, a representative of the Investigation claimed that the planted or "swapped" circuit board fragment the Prosecution brought to trial, had never been tested for explosives residue for "budgetary reasons."[174]

There was zero direct evidence that al-Megrahi loaded a bomb on Pan Am 103, the feeder flights to Pan Am 103—or aboard any plane. Nor did the Prosecution ever cogently suggest, let alone prove, how al-Megrahi could have remote controlled an unaccompanied suitcase-embedded bomb through the electronic security systems of three international airports, without any inside help. The very evidence that was used to prove al-Megrahi bought the Malta-purchased shirt supposedly found in the wreckage, proved that that supposition was implausible, if not inconceivable. The Prosecutor attempted to connect the Libyan al-Megrahi to the crime by the claim that the bomb used in the attack was built by Libyans, with bomb components supplied to the Libyans. Yet, the putative evidence that the bomb used to destroy Pan Am 103 came from materials supplied to the Libyans, was palpably manufactured and planted.

Nevertheless, under the vigilant watch of the international political and intelligence communities, the three-Judge Scottish Panel found Megrahi guilty of 270 counts of murder and sentenced him to life imprisonment on January 31, 2001. The court found co-defendant, Lamin Kahalifah Fhimah, not guilty.

Robert Black QC, an Edinburgh University professor emeritus of Scottish law, protested, "No reasonable tribunal, on the evidence heard at the original trial, should or could have convicted him and it is an absolute disgrace and outrage what the Scottish court did."[175] The Court acknowledged that witnesses had "openly lied to the court."[176] Gareth Peirce noted that "[Austrian Professor] Dr. Köchler, the UN's observer throughout the trial, recorded that [Edwin] Bollier [owner of the Swiss Bomb Maker, Mebo] had been 'brusquely interrupted' by the presiding judge when he attempted to raise the issue of the possible manipulation of the timer fragments."[177] Köchler proclaimed, "You cannot come out with a verdict of guilty for one and innocent for the other when they were both being tried with the same evidence."[178] Noting the political pressure applied upon the Judges during trial, Köchler observed that "proper judicial procedure is simply impossible if political interests and intelligence services – from whichever side – succeed in interfering in the actual conduct of a court."[179] Ultimately, Köchler announced, the court decisions constituted a "spectacular miscarriage of justice."[180]

Al-Megrahi was released on "compassionate" grounds on August 20, 2009, at the directive of Scottish Cabinet Secretary for Justice, Kenny MacAskill. On the face of it, al-Megrahi, who had terminal cancer, was released to alleviate his suffering and allow him to die at home. In reality, his release, like his original conviction, was driven by politics. When it became expedient for the West to build alliances with Syria and Iran in the Iraq war, the prosecution took an abrupt U-turn away from the actual culprits— Jibril, the PLFP-G.C., Iran and Syria, and towards the pariah and the scapegoat— Libya and al-Megrahi.

When the imminent prosecution of al-Megrahi's second appeal threatened to expose the falsification of evidence at the first trial and the real CIA, Iran and Syrian connections to the bombing; and when England and British Petroleum became eager for trade deals with Libya; al-

Megrahi was released. The investigation of the bombing, the conviction of al-Megrahi and ultimately his release were driven not by evidence, but by international politics, and the corrupt machinations of intelligence agencies.

Where was Mueller in all this? Leading the FBI in one of the most monumental investigations in the history of the Bureau. As Kevin Ryan records, "Mueller was . . . appointed as chief investigator of the . . . bombing of Pan Am 103 . . . ."[181] This was an investigation that, under Mueller's leadership, overlooked a mountain of evidence— the Iranian payments to Jibril before and after the crime for bombing an American plane; Jibril's use of an airport drug smuggling route developed by CIA asset, al-Kassar, and protected by the CIA, to plant a bomb on Pan Am 103; the arrest of Jibril's cell members in Frankfurt a few months before the attack, with one bomb like the one later used to destroy Pan Am 103, and the discovery that Jibril's group had a second bomb like the one later used to decimate Pan Am 103, that was still at large; Jibril's several admissions of guilt for the bombing; the CIA's tipoff to the Iranians that McKee was flying on Pan Am 103, and the go ahead by a CIA Control for the lethal mission to proceed. Mueller led an investigation that brazenly bribed witnesses, lied, discarded evidence, fabricated evidence, elevated political expedience over truth.

What was Mueller's move in leading a far-reaching coverup of the facts underlying the Pan Am bombing? Was it Mueller's motive to conceal the rogue CIA COREA Program that was smuggling heroin into America? Was it Mueller's motive to conceal the CIA's ties to international terrorists, arms dealers and drug traffickers? Was it his aim to hide the willingness of rogue CIA elements to condone the murder of innocent men, women and children, to cover up its own corruption?

What is known, is that Mueller presided over a systematic effort to conceal the international crimes that culminated in the destruction of Pan Am 103.

It is also known what Mueller did not do.

Mueller did not bring to justice al-Kassar, the international drug dealer, who transported heroin into America, and created the airport smuggling route that was apparently used to get a bomb on board Pan Am 103.

Mueller did not bring to justice Ahmed Jibril, the terrorist that was paid to bomb Pan Am 103 and bragged about doing it.

Mueller did not bring to justice the CIA agents who helped smuggle heroin into America, or the CIA agents who notified the Iranians that McKee and his team were flying on Pan Am 103.

Mueller did not bring to justice the CIA Controls who, according to INTEFOR, gave the go ahead for the flight— and its deadly cargo— to proceed.

Certainly, he did not achieve Justice for Charles McKee and his loyal team of federal agents who died aboard Pan Am 103, the eleven Scots in Lockerbie who were killed on the ground, and the over two hundred other innocents who perished in the explosion.

Chapter 4

BCCI

The Bank of Credit and Commerce International (BCCI) achieved worldwide notoriety in the 1980s, as the financier and money launderer for financial fraud, international drug trafficking, terrorism, illegal arms sales and CIA black ops. BCCI, according to observers, stole $10 billion from depositors, bribed politicians, helped corrupt the world's banking system.

William Safire provided a direct assessment of BCCI in the pages of the New York Times on July 21, 1991:

> The BCCI scandal involves the laundering of drug money, the illicit financing of terrorism and of arms to Iraq, the easy purchase of respectability and the corruption of the world banking system.
>
> For more than a decade, the biggest banking swindle in history worked beautifully. Between $5 billion and $15 billion was bilked from governments and individual depositors to be put to the most evil of purposes— while lawmen and regulators slept.[182]

A similar description was given in an op-ed by Muriel Kane, published by the *Wall Street Journal* over 17 years later on May 26, 2009:

> The BCCI scandal was the most important corruption story of the 20th century. Crooked

international bankers cast a world-wide web of influence. They bought and sold politicians around the globe, ripped off depositors for some $10 billion, laundered drug money, worked with assorted spooks and trafficked with terrorists . . . .[183]

Mueller, far from diligently investigating and prosecuting BCCI's abuses, obstructed the efforts of other law enforcement agencies and prosecutors to investigate BCCI. As stated by researcher Kevin Ryan, Mueller was brought in to oversee the BCCI investigation precisely because of his known propensity for cover-ups in instances of governmental wrongdoing.[184] Thus, Mueller was appointed Director of the Criminal Division of the Justice Department in 1990, served in that position from 1990 to 1993, and was in charge of the major decisions concerning the investigation and prosecution of BCCI principals. As Ryan further notes, BCCI became another one of Mueller's signature cover-ups:

> Mueller's talents were noticed early in his career at the Justice Department. . . . .
>
> Mueller was then appointed as chief investigator of the 1988 bombing of Pan Am 103 in Scotland. The account Mueller produced was a flimsy story that accused a Libyan named Megrahi of coordinating placement of a suitcase bomb that allegedly traveled unaccompanied through several airports to find its way to the doomed flight. . . . .
>
> With the Pan Am 103 case, Mueller was covering up facts related to some of the of victims of the bombing—a group of U.S.

intelligence specialists led by Major Charles McKee of the Defense Intelligence Agency. McKee had gone to Beirut to find and rescue hostages and, while there, learned about CIA involvement in a drug smuggling operation run through an agency project called COREA. As *TIME magazine reported*, the likely explanation for the bombing, supported by independent intelligence experts, was that U.S. operatives "targeted Flight 103 in order to kill the hostage-rescue team." This would prevent disclosure of what McKee's team had learned. That theory was also supported by the fact that the CIA showed up immediately at the scene of the crash, took McKee's briefcase, and returned it empty.

Mueller's diversions led to his leadership of the Criminal Division at the U.S. Department of Justice, putting him in charge of investigations regarding BCCI. . . . .

But again, Mueller was simply brought in to accomplish the cover-up. The facts were that BCCI was used by the CIA to operate outside of the rule of law through funding of terrorists and other criminal operatives. The bank network was at the root of some of the greatest crimes against the public in the last 50 years, including the Savings & Loan scandal, the Iran-Contra affair, and the creation of the al-Qaeda terrorist network.

Mueller was instrumental in obstructing the BCCI investigation led by Manhattan

District Attorney Robert Morgenthau. During this time, Justice Department prosecutors were instructed not to cooperate with Morgenthau. Describing Mueller's obstruction of Morgenthau, the *Wall Street Journal* reported that, "documents were withheld, and attempts were made to block other federal agencies from cooperating."[185]

Chris Floyd reported for *Counterpunch* on January 31, 2003, that Mueller was called in by President George H. W. Bush to direct the federal investigation of BCCI, when several prosecutors began to actively go after BCCI, and insiders got nervous.[186] In short, Mueller was brought in to protect wrongdoers involved in BCCI, not prosecute them. Mueller, as expected, swept national and international crimes under the rug, to the benefit of crooked insiders. As Floyd wrote: "When a few prosecutors finally began targeting BCCI's operations in the late Eighties," President George H. W. Bush "moved in with a federal probe directed by Justice Department investigator Robert Mueller." Mueller thus ascended to head the Justice Department's Criminal Division from 1990 to 1993. As noted by Muriel Kane, "When it came to making decisions about investigations and prosecutions in the BCCI affair [Mueller and Deputy Attorney General George Terwilliger] were the men at the switches . . . ."[187]

Manhattan District Attorney Robert Morgenthau was perhaps the prosecutor who most aggressively targeted the global financial fraud network embodied by BCCI. Instead of going after BCCI, Mueller set out to sabotage the efforts of the one prosecutor in America, Morgenthau, who took the lead in the effort to hold BCCI's principals accountable. As noted in the *Wall Street Journal*, "According to news reports over the years, Justice prosecutors were instructed not to cooperate with Mr. Morgenthau's office, documents were withheld, and attempts were made to block other federal agencies from cooperating."[188]

As Reporter Chris Floyd similarly recorded, "The U.S. Senate later found that the probe had been unaccountably 'botched'—witnesses went missing, CIA records got 'lost,' . . . Lower ranking prosecutors told of heavy pressure from on high to 'lay off.' Most of the big BCCI players went unpunished or, like [Khalid bin] Mahfouz, got off with wrist-slap fines and sanctions."[189]

As Barbara Boyd notes, Mueller, as the head of the Justice Department's Criminal Division, covered up international crimes, concealed corrupt black ops by intelligence agencies on both sides of the Atlantic— and kept well-connected conspirators out of jail. Thus, Boyd notes, Mueller

> successfully covered up the drug, weapons, and terrorism activities of two banks, BCCI and BNL. BCCI was the Anglo-American intelligence community's chosen vehicle to fund terrorism, launder drug money, and fund dark intelligence activities in Afghanistan, Central America, and throughout the Middle East. The highest levels of the British and European oligarchies were directly implicated in BCCI's activities. Both banks escaped with plea bargains and fines, protecting dirty state secrets on several continents from public disclosure.[190]

Chapter 5

Ruby Ridge

Randy Weaver, his wife, Vicki, and their children, moved to mountainous Ruby Ridge, Idaho in the early 1980s, where they bought 20 acres, and built a cabin to raise their children. Weaver reportedly attended several Aryan Nation meetings, but he and his wife declined to join the group, because of the Weavers' religious beliefs.

In 1985, the U.S. Secret Service and the FBI commenced a series of periodic interviews of, and contacts with, Weaver and his wife, Vicki.

In 1989, Weaver sold two modified shotguns to an undercover ATF agent. ATF later charged that the shotgun barrels were illegally shortened. Weaver has consistently maintained that the guns were of legal length when he conveyed them to the ATF undercover agent.

In the late 1980s, the ATF undercover agent asked Weaver to illegally cut the length of a shotgun barrel. The purpose of the ATF request was to enable the federal government to bring criminal charges against Weaver, and to use those charges as leverage to coerce Weaver to become an undercover agent for the federal government in their investigation of separatist groups. Weaver refused to cut the shotgun barrel as the undercover ATF agent asked him to do. In November 1989, Weaver refused to take the ATF agent to a meeting of "separatists" in Montana.

In June of 1990, there were no federal charges against Weaver. However, ATF Agents told Weaver that they would file charges against him for illegal weapons, if he did not become an undercover agent for them, and infiltrate the Aryan Nations group, of which Weaver was not a member. In effect, federal agents threatened to bring false federal criminal charges against Weaver, if he did not become an uncover agent for them. Weaver again refused to become an undercover agent for federal agencies.

Because of Weaver's refusal to become an undercover agent for the federal government, the ATF arrested him in January 1991, for transferring a short-barreled shotgun without a license. Again, Weaver had already declined to illegally shorten a shotgun barrel at the request of an undercover agent; Weaver maintained that the shotguns transferred by him to federal agents were of legal dimensions; and it was the federal undercover operatives, not Weaver, who had initiated the shotgun transfers. Federal Pretrial Services sent a Notice to Weaver with the wrong court date— March 20, 1991. The U.S. Attorney then sought a Grand Jury indictment of Weaver on March 14, 1991, charging Weaver with failure to appear for Court. The U.S. Attorney sought an indictment of Weaver on March 14, for failing to appear for court, even though the Court Notice sent to Weaver ordered him to be in court on March 20, and March 20 had not yet arrived.

At this point, Weaver had been wrongfully charged with transferring an illegally shortened shotgun, though he had not done this; and the U.S. Attorney had sought to indict him for failure to appear for court, even though the Court date provided him by the Court had not yet arrived. These actions led the Weavers, who had no lawyer, to believe that they had no chance of getting fair treatment in federal proceedings.

In October 1991, the Weavers agreed with the Marshall's service to voluntarily surrender. The U.S. Attorney revoked the agreement. The Marshalls' Office then recommended that the indictment be dismissed and refiled under seal, so Weaver would drop his guard, and could be arrested without incident. Again, the U.S. Attorney nixed this possibility of a peaceful resolution.

On August 21, 1992, several Deputy U.S. Marshalls went to the Weavers' property to reconnoiter it. The Weavers' dogs began to bark. The Weavers' 14-year-old son, Sammy, and Kevin Harris, a 24-year-old family friend, went out with guns to investigate. The deputy marshals contend that they were first fired on by Sammy and Kevin Harris. Randy Weaver and Kevin Harris consistently contended that the camouflaged marshals fired first without identifying themselves— and without Sammy Weaver and Harris even knowing who was shooting at them. A federal agent, Bill Deegan, was mortally wounded. Fourteen-year-old Sammy was shot in the back with a submachine gun by a federal agent and killed, while running away from the encounter, toward his family's home.

On August 22, 1992, FBI officers assembled on the north ridge overlooking the cabin. They did not request a surrender or announce their presence. The Weavers had retrieved the body of their 14-year-old son, Sammy, who had been killed the day before, and had placed his body in a shed near their cabin. That same day, August 22, 1992, Randy Weaver walked out of his cabin, unarmed, to view the body of his 14-year-old son. His 16-year-old daughter, Sara, and the family friend, Kevin Harris, were also with him. As Randy Weaver was looking at the body of his son, Weaver's back was toward FBI Sniper, Lon Horiuchi. Sniper Horiuchi fired at Weaver's back, in an attempt to sever Weaver's spine, and instantly kill him. Randy Weaver moved at the last instant, and the bullet struck Weaver in the shoulder. Randy Weaver, his daughter Sara and Kevin Harris ran for their cabin. Horiuchi fired a second shot, striking Randy Weaver's wife, Vicki, in the head, as she stood unarmed in the door of their home, holding her 10-month-old, infant daughter. Vicki Weaver died instantly.

Later— after 14-year-old Sammy Weaver, 43-year-old Vicki Weaver, and a federal agent had all been killed— a robot vehicle approached the cabin and announced the presence of law enforcement. According to the Weavers, this was the first time that the presence of federal law enforcement, and the source of the gunfire, had been revealed.

For the next ten days, 350 to 400 federal agents surrounded the Weavers' cabin. Inside the cabin were Randy Weaver, his three surviving children, family friend Kevin Harris, and the body of his wife, Vicki, under a blood-soaked blanket. The government force named their temporary camp, "Camp Vicki". Each morning, the federal negotiators would call out to the survivors, "Vicki, we have blueberry pancakes." Weaver gave up, after radio commentator Paul Harvey intervened, and assured he would pay for a legal defense.

Ultimately, Randy Weaver's alleged crimes consisted of attending several Aryan meetings, before deciding against joining; purportedly selling a shotgun that was alleged to be illegally short, which Weaver has always denied, in a transaction that was initiated by federal agents not Weaver; and missing a court date after receiving an Appearance Notice with the wrong date. His real offense in the eyes of the federal agents? Refusing to do undercover work for the ATF.

For these purported crimes, Weaver's 14-year-old son and wife were shot to death by federal agents at Ruby Ridge. Ultimately, Weaver was acquitted of all charges except failure to appear for court; Kevin Harris was acquitted of all criminal charges.

In 1997, the District Attorney for Boundary County, Idaho, charged FBI sniper Horiuchi with involuntary manslaughter, for shooting Vicki Weaver to death, as she stood unarmed in the doorway of the family cabin holding her 10-month old daughter. The U.S. Attorney for the District of Idaho intervened and dismissed the charges.

Earlier, in October 1991, the United States Marshall for the Idaho District and the Weavers had reached an agreement for Randy Weaver to peacefully and voluntarily surrender himself. If that deal had been carried out, it would have spared the lives of Vicki Weaver, her 14-year-old son, Sammy, and United States Deputy Marshall, Bill Deegan. However, the acting U.S. Attorney revoked the deal between the Marshall's Office and the Weavers, for the Weavers' peaceful surrender. Robert Mueller was the Director of the Criminal Division of the Department of Justice at the time the local U.S. Attorney revoked the agreement for the peaceful surrender of Randy Weaver.

After the shooting of Vicki Weaver, Sammy Weaver and Randy Weaver, Robert Mueller was incensed. Not because a federal sniper had shot and killed an unarmed woman in the head, while she was holding her infant child in the doorway of her own home. Not because one or more federal agents had shot and killed her 14-year-old son by shooting him in the back with a submachine gun, while he was running away from gunfire. Not because a federal agent shot Randy Weaver in the back, when he was unarmed, and tried to kill him.

Robert Mueller was furious, instead, because members of Congress, and public officials dared complain when an FBI sniper shot Vicki Weaver in the head and killed her son. At the time, in 1992, Mueller headed the Criminal Division of the Justice Department. As Neil A. Lewis reported for *The New York Times*, "(Mueller's) Associates recall his anger at members of Congress and others for criticism of the FBI's siege of a separatist family at Ruby Ridge in Idaho, where a woman, her 14 year old son and a deputy United States marshal were killed."[191]

Chapter 6

9-11

President George W. Bush named Mueller Director of the FBI in 2001. Mueller took control of the FBI on September 4, 2001— one week before 9-11. Mueller, well-schooled in covert operations, did not hesitate. As Kevin Ryan has summarized,

> Under Mueller, the FBI began the whitewash of 9/11 immediately. Mueller himself lied repeatedly in the direct aftermath with respect to FBI knowledge of the accused hijackers. He claimed that the alleged hijackers left no paper trail, and suggested that they exercised "extraordinary secrecy" and "discipline never broke down." . . . .
>
> Meanwhile, Mueller's FBI immediately seized control of the investigations at the World Trade Center, the Pentagon, and in Shanksville, PA where United Flight 93 was destroyed. Under Mueller, leaders of the Bureau went on to arrest and intimidate witnesses, destroy or withhold evidence, and prevent any independent investigation. With Mueller in the lead, the FBI failed to cooperate with the government investigations into 9/11 and failed miserably to perform basic investigatory tasks. Instead, Mueller celebrated some of the most egregious pre-9/11 failures of the FBI by giving those involved promotions, awards, and cash bonuses.[192]

As a first priority, after 9-11, Mueller's FBI helped facilitate an airlift of Saudis— including bin Ladens— out of America. *CBS News* reported on September 30, 2001, citing comments by the Saudi ambassador to Washington, that two dozen members of Osama bin Laden's family were quickly flown out of America several days after 9-11.[193]   Further, young members of the bin Laden family were taken to a secret location in Texas, under FBI supervision. According to the CBS report, the bin Laden family members were flown out of the United States on a private charter when American airports reopened 3 days after the attack on the World Trade Center.[194]

Craig Unger, the author of *House of Bush, House of Saud*, recorded that "there were at least eight planes stopping in 12 U.S. cities to fly Saudis out. About two dozen passengers were related to [Osama] Bin Laden."[195] Ruminating on the evacuation,   Unger noted that "U.S. intelligence knew that 15 of the 19 hijackers were Saudi."[196] Moreover, "the most astonishing name" on the list of sudden Saudi evacuees, was the late Prince Ahmed Salman who, according to "Why America Slept," had alleged ties to Al Qaeda and advance knowledge of a major attack on America on 9-11. The fact of the evacuation, and the identity of the evacuees, said Unger "leaves the questions of why the FBI did not appear to be interested in Salman or the Bin Laden relatives or the others on the flight, and why the White House went to such great lengths to expedite the departure of a potential treasure trove of intelligence."[197] Concluded Unger, "The 9-11 commission should ask FBI Director Robert Mueller and Atty. Gen. John Ashcroft why such a man [Salman] was allowed to leave the country immediately after the attacks."[198]

Post 9-11, Mueller essentially claimed that the American Government had no forewarning or clues about the attack on the World Trade Center. Mueller commented on the Government's alleged lack of pre-9-11 clues, in a speech to the Commonwealth Club in San Francisco on April 19, 2002, the text of which was released by the FBI. According to Mueller, the hijackers "left no paper trail;"[199] "[i]n our investigation, we have not uncovered a single piece of paper;"[200] the hijackers used "meticulous planning, extraordinary secrecy" to conceal their plot;[201] and the "terrorists had managed . . . to stay out of sight, and to not let anyone know what they were up to beyond a very closed circle."[202]

Mueller's claim that the Government had no forewarning of the attack is irreconcilable with the facts. Some of the many red flags, red alerts and forewarnings:

On or about May 15, 2002, FBI officials acknowledged that, "The F.B.I. knew by 1996 of a specific threat that terrorists in Al Qaeda, Mr. bin Laden's network, might use a plane in a suicide attack against the headquarters of the C.I.A. or another large federal building in the Washington area," reported Phillip Shenon on May 18, 2002.[203]

"Six years before the Sept. 11 attacks, the CIA warned in a classified report that Islamic extremists likely would strike on U.S. soil at landmarks in Washington or New York, or through the airline industry, according to intelligence officials," reported Rebecca Leung with CBS/AP on March 21, 2004.[204]

"Twenty months before the Sept. 11 attacks, the CIA tracked two of the would-be hijackers as possible al Qaeda terrorists, but delayed alerting other government agencies that could have blocked their entry to the United States or spied on them once they arrived," reported Zachary Coile on June 3, 2002.[205]

"White House officials acknowledged that U.S. intelligence officials informed President Bush weeks before the Sept. 11 attacks that bin Laden's terrorist network might try to hijack American planes, and that information prompted administration officials to issue a private warning to transportation officials and national security agencies," reported Terry Moran, Linda Douglass, Brian Ross and Lisa Sylvester of *ABC News* on May 16, 2002. They went on to state, "Two months before the hijackings, FBI agents in Phoenix reported their suspicions about Arab students at a Phoenix flight school, and directly referred to the possibility of a connection to bin Laden."[206]

As reported by Jason Burke and Ed Vulliamy of *The Guardian* on May 18, 2002, "George Bush received specific warnings in the weeks before 11 September that an attack inside the United States was being planned by Osama bin Laden's al-Qaeda network, US government sources said [May 17, 2002]."[207]

"Five days before Sept. 11, National Security Advisor Condoleezza Rice was warned that a terrorist attack inside the United States was imminent, a former U.S. Senator [Senator Gary Hart] who headed up a blue-ribbon commission on terrorism revealed late Tuesday [May 28, 2002]," according to Carl Limbacher of *News Max* on May 29, 2002.[208]

According to Kurt Eichenwald of *The New York Times*,

On Aug. 6, 2001, President George W. Bush received a classified review of the threats posed by Osama bin Laden and his terrorist network, Al Qaeda. That morning's "presidential daily brief" — the top-secret document prepared by America's intelligence agencies — featured the now-infamous heading: "Bin Laden Determined to Strike in U.S." A few weeks later, on 9/11, Al Qaeda accomplished that goal.[209]

As Eichenwald further stated, "It was perhaps the most famous presidential briefing in history."[210]

Jamie Holguin with *CBS News* reported on June 2, 2002 that Assistant Attorney General Michael Chertoff stated on Friday May 31, 2002 in a commencement speech to Seton Hall Law School graduates, "As of Sept. 10th, each of us knew everything we needed to know to tell us there was a possibility of what happened on Sept. 11th."[211]

Max Cleland is the former U.S. Senator from Georgia, and former member of the 9-11 Commission, who resigned from the Commission in December 2003, over his concerns that the President George W. Bush White House was covering up the events of 9-11. In October 2003, Cleland charged that "As each day goes by, we learn that this government knew a whole lot more about these terrorists before September 11 than it has ever admitted."[212]

Colleen Rowley is the former FBI special agent and division counsel, and whistleblower, who was named one of TIME's "Persons of the Year" in 2002. Rowley sent a May 2002 Memo to Robert Mueller that set forth the FBI's pre-9-11 failures. Rowley also disputes Mueller's denial of forewarning. In a televised Interview in 2017 with *The Real News*, Rowley bluntly stated: "The FBI and all the other officials claimed that there were no clues, that they had no warning etc., and that was not the case. There had been all kinds of memos and intelligence coming in."[213]

When Robert Mueller states the American Government and intelligence establishment had no forewarning of the 9-11 attacks, what he really means is that *the American people* had no forewarning of 9-11.

Moreover, Mueller not only misrepresented that the government received no prior warnings about 9-11. Mueller actively intervened to prevent post-9-11 investigations from uncovering and proving that the government had in fact received prior warnings about 9-11. Mueller strove to coverup that federal security agencies had specific intelligence about the hijackers before 9-11, and Mueller attempted to conceal the abundance of pre-9-11 warnings received by government and intelligence officials.

Before September, 2001, two of the 9-11 Saudi hijackers were provided money, shelter and connections in San Diego, by a paid FBI informant, and by a network of Saudis, living in America, that included Saudi Officials. Mueller attempted to cover up the connection between the Saudi hijackers, on the one hand, and the FBI informant and Saudi Government officials on the other.

The Joint Inquiry into Intelligence Community Activities Before and After the Terrorist Attacks of September 11, 2001 ("Joint Inquiry"), was a Congressional Inquiry conducted by the Senate Select Committee on Intelligence and the House Permanent Select Committee on Intelligence. This Joint Congressional Inquiry ("Joint

Inquiry") commenced in February of 2002 and rendered a formal report in December 2002.

Andrew Cockburn of *Harper's* detailed the daring efforts of at least one Joint Inquiry Investigator to chase down West Coast leads on the 9-11 attacks.[214] As Cockburn has reported, in 2002, Joint Inquiry Investigator, and former FBI analyst, Michael Jacobson, found a reference in FBI files that stated an FBI informant in San Diego knew one of the hijackers.[215] Jacobson decided to go to San Diego to investigate the connection between the FBI informant and the Saudi hijackers.

By February 2000, two of the Saudi terrorists, Nawaf al-Hazmi and Khalid al-Mihdhar had flown from Malaysia to Los Angeles. After Joint Inquiry Investigator Jacobson flew to San Diego in 2002, Jacobson discovered that about two weeks after the two Saudi terrorists, al-Hazmi and al-Mihdhar, arrived in Los Angeles in early 2000, Saudi asset, Omar al-Bayoumi, met with a Saudi Muslim cleric, Fahad al-Thumairy. Al-Thumairy was later banned from the United States for his jihad connections.

After meeting with Al-Thumairy, Al-Bayoumi began working as a handler for the two Saudi terrorists, al-Hazmi and al-Mihdhar. As Cockburn reported, al-Bayoumi "invited [the two Saudi terrorists] to move to San Diego, found them an apartment, paid their first month's rent, helped them open a bank account, and introduced them to members of the local Saudi community."[216] Al-Bayoumi, himself a Saudi asset, had "a no-show job at a local company with connections to the Saudi Ministry of Defense and Aviation." Al-Bayoumi got paid by his employer without working. Moreover, as Cockburn reports, "During the time Bayoumi was catering to the hijackers' needs, his salary as a ghost employee of the aviation company got a 700 percent boost; it was cut when they left town."[217]

Al-Bayoumi, the handler of the Saudi hijackers, got other help from the Saudis. Thus, one of the Saudis living in the San Diego area, began signing over to Bayoumi, checks received from the wife of the Saudi ambassador in Washington. One of the Saudi terrorists "had worked for a San Diego businessman who had himself been the subject of an FBI counterterrorism investigation." [218]

"Even more amazingly," reports Cockburn, "the two hijackers had been close with an FBI informant, Adbusattar Shaikh."[219] One of the hijackers lived with Shaikh for a period of time before 9-11.

The 2002 inquiry in San Diego by Jacobson and other Joint Inquiry members yielded other fruit— admissions by federal agents that the Saudi Government assisted the terrorists that perpetrated the 9-11 attack. As Cockburn reports,

> Another intriguing document unearthed by the investigators in San Diego was a memo from July 2, 2002, discussing alleged financial connections between the September 11 hijackers, Saudi government officials, and members of the Saudi royal family. It stated that there was "incontrovertible evidence that there is support for these terrorists within the Saudi Government."[220]

In short, the on-site inquiry in San Diego proved that the Saudi Government was hosting, aiding and bankrolling the terrorists through handlers and intermediaries— and that a paid FBI informant provided one of the hijackers a place to live.

Mueller tried to derail the Joint Inquiry's Investigative reconnaissance in San Diego. Bob Graham is a former U.S. Senator from Florida, and former Chair of the Senate Intelligence Committee, who served as co-Chair of the Congressional Joint Inquiry into 9-11 ("Joint Inquiry"). Former Senator Graham stated in 2017 that Mueller personally intervened to try to stop Jacobson from going to San Diego to investigate the ties between two Saudi 9-11 hijackers, on the one hand, and an FBI informant and Saudi Government officials on the other. Reports Cockburn:

> Bob Graham, the former chairman of the Senate Intelligence Committee, told me recently that Robert Mueller, then the FBI director . . . made "the strongest objections" to Jacobson and his colleagues visiting San Diego.[221]

Thus, when Jacobson and his colleagues flew west, they "defied Mueller's efforts."[222]

As further reported by Cockburn, when investigators for the Congressional Joint Inquiry discovered that a paid FBI informant, Shaikh, had hosted, and rented a room, to a hijacker in 2000, the FBI "refused outright" to allow the informant, Shaikh, to be interviewed, and "hid him in an unknown location." The move, they said, was "for his own safety." In short, the FBI secreted their own informant so that the Joint Inquiry could not question him about Saudi or federal connections to the 9-11 hijackers, or the events of 9-11. Senator Graham later wrote that the FBI "insisted that we could not, even in the most sanitized manner, tell the

American people that an FBI informant had a relationship with two of the hijackers."[223]

The Joint Inquiry, as Cockburn summarizes, "uncovered numerous failures by the FBI and CIA," a "degree of cumulative incompetence [that] was breathtaking."[224] Nawaf al-Hazmi and Khalid al-Mihdhar were the two hijackers who flew to California in February 2000, and were hosted by Saudi operative al-Bayoumi and FBI informant Shaikh. As Cockburn notes,

> Most egregiously, the CIA had been well aware that two known Al Qaeda operatives, Nawaf al-Hazmi and Khalid al-Mihdhar [the two Saudi terrorists who flew to California and were hosted by al-Bayoumi and FBI Informant Shaikh,] were en route to the United States, but the agency had refused to tell the FBI. The FBI, meanwhile, had multiple reports in its San Diego office on locally based Saudis suspected of terrorist associations, but failed to take action.[225]

Mueller intervened, and tried to short circuit the San Diego inquiry that documented the ties between the 9-11 hijackers on the one hand, and the Saudi government and a paid FBI informant, on the other. Mueller attempted to conceal the fact that the FBI knew in advance of the hijackers' presence on American soil— and yet did not move to stop the attack.

Mueller made other efforts to obstruct the investigation of 9-11. The "Joint Inquiry" was conducted by the relevant Senate Select Committee on Intelligence and the House Permanent Select Committee on Intelligence. The 9-11

Commission, on the other hand, was created by Congressional legislation, and was established November 27, 2002 by President George W. Bush and Congress, to investigate 9-11. The 9-11 Commission members were chosen by President George W. Bush and Congress, and had eleven members.

Former FBI Agent and whistleblower, Colleen Rowley, has stated that the FBI, under Mueller, sent "Soviet-style minders" to her formal interviews with the 9-11 Commission to help ensure that she didn't say anything of which the FBI did not approve. A 9-11 Commission memo complained that "Minders" actually answered questions directed to the witnesses. According to a 2003 Article in the *New York Times*, both co-chairs of the 9/11 Commission indicated that government "minders"[226] obstructed the investigation into 9-11 by intimidating witnesses.

FBI Special Agents Robert Wright and John Vincent, of the FBI's Counter-Terrorism Office in Chicago, uncovered Saudi money laundering into and in the United States in the months before 9-11, and both believed that a massive terrorist attack was imminent. Moreover, during their investigation, they asked a fellow agent of Muslim descent, to go undercover with a wire to obtain more evidence of the ongoing Saudi conspiracy. The Muslim agent refused, in effect asserting his allegiance to fellow Muslims over his allegiance to the Bureau. Wright and Vincent reported to their FBI Supervisors, that the Agent was unwilling to go undercover in their investigation of the Saudis,. The FBI Supervisors not only did nothing about the Muslim Agent's unwillingness to assist in the investigation of the Saudis. The Supervisors also pulled the plug on the investigation by

Agents Wright and Vincent into the Saudi operations on American soil.

According to Larry Klayman, counsel for Wright and Vincent, "Mueller later led an effort to drum both Special Agents Wright and Vincent out of the FBI, in part by removing their security clearances, as a 'reward' for their candor." While Mueller punished honest Agents that attempted to prevent terrorist attacks on American soil, he "celebrated some of the most egregious pre-9-11 failures of the FBI by giving those involved promotions, awards and cash bonuses."[227]

Jon Kreindler, the attorney for families of victims suing the Saudis for the attack on 9-11, gave an Interview to *InfoWars* that was broadcast on July 7, 2018. In that interview, Kreindler denounced the systematic obstruction, by the Bush White House and Robert Mueller, of the investigation into the Saudis' involvement in 9-11. As Kreindler protested:

> [There is a] [h]uge body of evidence that Saudi Government officials prepared for the hijackers' arrival, helped them, got them money, English lessons, safehouses and apartments, and provided the aid without which it would have been impossible, according to the FBI agents who were working the case, for the terrorists to succeed. And President Bush and Director Mueller, instead of furthering that effort to find the whole story, quashed it. Interrogations were shut down. Documents were kept secret.[228]

On October 9, 2002, Mueller testified before Congress that facts concerning the Saudi orchestration of 9-11 came to his attention *as a result of the post 9-11 Joint Inquiry*— in effect that Mueller didn't know about the Saudi involvement in 9-11, until the Joint Inquiry told him about it. As Mueller testified, "some facts [concerning Saudi involvement] came to light here and to me, frankly, that had not come to light before, and perhaps would not have come to light had the staff not probed."[229]

In fact, contrary to Mueller's attempt to convince Congress that he did not know about the Saudi connection to 9-11, he and the FBI command structure tried to coverup the Saudis involvement in 9-11. Thus, Mueller's FBI actively worked to prohibit the FBI's own field agents from investigating and proving Saudi involvement. As Eric Zuesse of Strategic Culture Foundation wrote on July 11, 2017, Mueller had "squelched" the post 9-11 efforts of his field agents who "had been urgently trying to obtain . . . authorization to launch an intensive investigation into the . . . financing, and possible direction, of the 9/11 attacks, by top officials of the Saudi Government."[230]

In short, contrary to his pretended naivete about Saudi sponsorship of 9-11, Mueller had personally scrambled to stop his own Field Agents from investigating the actions of the Saudis in helping engineer the attacks of 9-11. Mueller denied knowing about a criminal conspiracy, that he himself, actively tried to conceal.

Mueller helped fly Saudis, including bin Ladens, out of America, in the days following 9-11; tried to prevent honest officials and agents from investigating the Saudis' involvement in 9-11; and concealed the involvement of Saudi Officials in funding and planning the attacks of 9-11. Yet, while he protected the guilty— he punished the innocent. Thus, after helping evacuate the bin Ladens and prominent Saudis from America in the wake of 9-11, Mueller authorized the round-up, detention and abuse of Middle Eastern immigrants in New York City— who had nothing to do with 9-11.

This conduct fits seamlessly with Mueller's pattern of protecting the guilty and persecuting the innocent. Moreover, Mueller attempted to gain favorable media coverage from his actions, representing that in detaining immigrants who had nothing to do with 9-11, the FBI was actively investigating the truth about 9-11.

As Barbara Boyd has reported, after "[Saudi] Prince Bandar had already moved the key Saudis involved with the hijackers out of the United States,"[231] Mueller and Attorney General John Ashcroft "rounded up 762 Muslims who had overstayed their visas . . . . These individuals were detained, without charges, in a special unit of New York's Metropolitan Detention Center. Their jail conditions were supervised by Mueller and a small group of other Washington officials . . . . They were deprived of sleep and food, repeatedly strip searched, physically and verbally abused by guards, and denied . . . any access to the outside world."[232]

Mueller's FBI actively participated in whisking Saudis, including the bin Ladens, out of America, in the days following 9-11. Mueller personally intervened to circumvent an inquest in San Diego into the connections between an FBI informant, Saudi officials and Saudi operatives on the one hand, and Saudi hijackers on the other hand. Mueller sent Soviet-style "Minders" to interviews conducted by the 9-11 Commission appointed by President George W. Bush, to inhibit witnesses and federal agents from speaking openly about the events preceding and succeeding 9-11; to prevent the revelation of the involvement of the Saudi Government; and to bury the fact that the federal government had evidence of a terrorist attack before 9-11— and did nothing to stop it. Mueller concealed the primacy of the role played by the Saudi Government in the attack. Mueller falsely denied that intelligence agencies and the federal government had advance warnings of 9-11. Mueller fraudulently attempted to conceal that federal agencies were tracking the hijackers' movements before 9-11, and possessed evidence of a looming terrorist attack before 9-11 occurred.

Mueller's actions point to a specific intent to conceal the involvement of the Saudi Government in 9-11. As 9-11 widow and now inveterate 9-11 Investigator, Kristen Breitweiser, states "Mueller and other FBI officials had purposely tried to keep any incriminating information specifically surrounding the Saudis out of the [Joint] Inquiry's investigative hands. To repeat, there was a concerted effort by the FBI and the Bush Administration to keep incriminating Saudi evidence out of the Inquiry's investigation."[233]

Mueller repeatedly endeavored to coverup the involvement of the Saudis in the criminal atrocity of 9-11. However, it's the Saudis that helped commit the crimes. When a detective refuses to investigate the prime suspect, it is difficult to solve the crime.

Ultimately, Mueller strove to conceal that intelligence agencies and the federal government had substantive evidence before 9-11 of an imminent terrorist attack— and top intelligence bureaucrats and government officials did nothing to stop it.

Why would Mueller try to coverup the Saudi ties to the crime? Is it because, given their strong ties to certain Americans, proof of Saudi involvement in 9-11 would indict elements of the American government for having foreknowledge of 9-11 and for the fact that they did nothing to stop it?

Moreover, **Saudi Arabia** was integrally involved in the 9-11 attack on America. Yet, America declared war— on **Iraq.** America declared war on **Iraq** in retribution for an attack perpetrated by **Saudi Arabia.** Did Mueller try to conceal Saudi involvement, to distract America from the political and military fact that the United States declared war on Iraq, for a crime committed by, among others, Saudi Arabia?

Prior to 9-11, John O'Neill led the FBI's counter-terrorism division. The O'Neill-led counter-terrorism division, was fighting the cyber and intelligence war against Al Qaeda. In 2001, O'Neill's team was working tirelessly to process the evidence of a growing effort by Al Qaeda to launch an attack on American soil. O'Neill pleaded for more resources, because the terrorist threat was growing, and O'Neill wanted to turn back the terrorists from their violent objectives. Mueller, then Deputy Attorney General, blocked a major funding increase for the O'Neill-led effort to wage the cyber and intelligence war against Al Qaeda. Incensed that "official Washington would not listen to his warnings about Al Qaeda," O'Neill moved his entire operation from Washington to New York.[234] O'Neill retired from the FBI in August 2001— arguably out of frustration over opposition from Mueller to O'Neill's efforts to monitor the terrorists' activities and prevent a terrorist attack. On 9-11, O'Neill was a Security Official at the World Trade Center.

As *WashingtonsBlog* reported on June 14, 2011, "9/11 family member and 'Jersey Girl' Patty Casazza was told by whistleblowers that— before 9/11— the government knew the exact *day*, the type of attack, and the *targets.*"[235]   John O'Neill had fought the Washington bureaucracy, to protect America against Al Qaeda. No one in government bothered to tell John O'Neill that they had exacting intelligence about the time and place of the strike. John O'Neill was in the World Trade Center South Tower on September 11— and paid for his service to his nation with his life.

The nearly 3,000 people that died on 9-11, included more than 400 New York City police officers and firefighters who rushed to the Scene and into the Towers, to rescue victims.   The police and firefighters themselves became casualties of a terrorist attack of which top officials had been forewarned— but did not prevent.

Chapter 7

Anthrax

Dr. Bruce Ivins, a scientific researcher, was seen as thoughtful, studious, hardworking, kind and honest by his colleagues at the U.S. Army Medical Research Institute for Infectious Diseases (USAMRIID) at Fort Detrick, Maryland. To be sure, he had his emotional scars. Growing up, the youngest of 3 boys, his mother had been violent and abusive to her children, intentionally attempting to abort his life, in a series of staged, traumatic falls, which he learned about later in life.

Dr. Ivins subsequently walked into another psychic ambush, for which he was not prepared, and which he did not precipitate. Working out his angst in his Catholic faith and seeking therapy, he chose a "therapist," who turned out to be an alcoholic and drug abuser, who after being cajoled or worse by the FBI, betrayed him, and publically and falsely denigrated him— before she herself disappeared. Bruce Ivins had the misfortune of seeking therapy from a misguided counselor. Unbeknownst to Ivins, when he sought her counseling, the counselor, Jean Duley, was a past or current drug addict, who once stated in a 1999 newspaper interview "Heroin. Cocaine. PCP. You name it, I did it."[236] Duley had charges for driving under the influence and battery upon her husband. After significant interaction with the FBI, Duley sold her patient out, violated Counselor-Patient confidentiality, and publicly demeaned him.

Bruce Ivins had a therapist who was willing to ingratiate herself with federal agents, sell out her Patient, breach confidentiality, put her own interests before those of her patient, and publicly malign him. The willingness of Ivins' therapist to engage in misconduct— and sell out her own patient— may have been the reason Mueller's FBI inquiry singled Bruce Ivins out, and publicly identified him, as the anthrax suspect. Ivins' malleable and immoral counselor made him an easy target: the FBI could publicly demonize him through his own counselor, before anyone even looked at the actual evidence.

In retrospect, Ivins may have ruminated over the notion that his life was destined to be a cosmic firefall. Yet, in his public accusation, in his death, in his uncharted ignominy, his scientific colleagues stood by him, virtually to a man, defending his honor— and innocence.

Following the 9-11 attacks in the fall of 2001, a series of mailings were sent that contained the poisonous spore, anthrax. Five Americans were killed in the attacks, 17 others sickened. On September 18, 2001, two of the anthrax mailings were sent to two news media outlets in New York City, the *New York Post* and Tom Brokaw at NBC. On October 9, 2001, anthrax mailings were also sent to two U.S. Senators in Washington, Patrick Leahy and Tom Daschle. It was believed that a fifth mailing was sent to American Media, Inc. (AMI) in Boca Raton, Florida where an AMI employee died from anthrax poisoning and heavy spore contamination in the building. The four envelopes sent to the New York media and U.S. Senators were recovered by authorities.

PENTTBOM (Pentagon/Twin Towers Bombing Investigation) is the Codename given by the FBI to its investigation of 9-11, the largest criminal inquest in the history of the FBI. Under traditional FBI procedures, investigations are conducted with some independence from the field Offices. Not so with the Anthrax inquiry— part of the FBI's "PENTTBOM" Investigation. Mueller, as the FBI Director, ordered that the investigation be directed from the Washington Field Office, so that he could have his own hands on the steering wheel. Mueller personally retained direct control of the anthrax investigation. This was to be a political, not evidentiary, investigation.

In October 2002, Mueller placed FBI Agent Richard Lambert nominally in charge of the Anthrax Investigation. Lambert attempted to lead the investigation for four years. Lambert ultimately filed a whistleblower complaint against the FBI, and a subsequent lawsuit, asserting that the FBI undermined, obstructed— and sabotaged— the inquiry into who was responsible for the Anthrax attacks. Lambert's first-hand direct experience in attempting to answer the question of who perpetrated the Anthrax attacks, refutes any notion that the FBI leadership ever wanted the truth to come out about who actually perpetrated the anthrax mailings. The FBI's Washington Field Office (WFO), the FBI's executive management and the FBI Laboratory resisted Lambert's efforts with roadblocks, hostility and manipulation.

As set forth by Lambert and detailed by *WashingtonsBlog*, the WFO persistently understaffed the anthrax investigation.[237] The WFO's Agent in Charge threatened to retaliate against Lambert, if Lambert notified FBI Headquarters of the understaffing. The WFO evicted the Anthrax task force from the WFO building in downtown Washington. Mueller ordered Lambert to "compartmentalize" the investigation, to reduce the amount of information known by each investigator. Mueller's ploy precluded investigators from viewing the totality of the evidence, and thus prevented them from connecting the dots, and grasping the big picture. Lambert believed this stratagem by Mueller reduced team morale.

The FBI transferred two Ph.D. Microbiologists from the team, to an 18-month Arabic language training program in Israel. The FBI Lab deliberately concealed, from Lambert's Task Force, its discovery of human DNA on the anthrax-laden envelope addressed to Senator Leahy— evidence that could have helped rule out innocent suspects or dramatically implicated guilty parties. The FBI Lab initially refused to perform comparison testing of the DNA sample. The FBI Lab, in Lambert's view, deliberately refused to provide prompt and competent scientific evaluations of the physical and biochemical evidence.

The FBI's pattern of foot-dragging, obstruction and subterfuge in the conduct of the investigation rendered it impossible for many outside observers to reconcile the FBI's actions and inaction with the notion that Mueller actually wanted or directed the FBI to reveal who was actually guilty of the Anthrax mailings.

The FBI not only subverted the operation of the investigation. The FBI also publicly accused Dr. Ivins of being the culprit, and ruined his life, based upon dubious evidence. Thus, Lambert also complained about the FBI's declaration, in 2008, that Dr. Bruce Ivins, a government scientist at Fort Detrick, Maryland, was the anthrax mailer, despite significant exculpatory evidence.

As set out by *WashingtonsBlog,* American laboratory scientists debunked the FBI's manufactured case against Ivins.[238] In the first instance, the killer anthrax was a hard to produce, dry powder form of the spore. However, the Fort Detrick, Maryland facility at which Dr. Ivins worked, handled only *liquid* anthrax. Other government labs in America— not Fort Detrick— produced *dry* anthrax.

Further, the anthrax used in the anthrax mailings, was characterized by a highly-specialized anti-static coating. Thus, the anthrax spores were coated with polyglass, creating an electrostatic charge, such that the anthrax spores would not clump, and would have a tendency to "float" in the air, and be available for the victim's inhalation. This highly weaponized form of anthrax represented extremely advanced bio-weapons technology. Ivins' bosses at Fort Detrick, who worked with him at the same lab every workday, stated Ivins did not have access to this type of highly developed bio-weapons application.

Furthermore, leading anthrax expert, Richard Spertzel, chief biological inspector for the U.N. Special Commission from 1994 to 1998, declares that Ivins didn't do it, because only 4 or 5 scientists in America knew how to make weaponized anthrax of the lethal quality used in the letters. Spertzel pronounced that, while the FBI claimed Dr. Ivins produced the weaponized, electrostatically charged, anthrax spores working a few nights alone, Spertzel stated it could have taken a top shelf expert on the spores— one of 4 or 5 in America— an entire year, with a full lab and a complete staff to produce the type of anthrax spores used in the post 9-11 attacks. As Spertzel has said, "In my opinion, there are maybe four or five people in the whole country who might be able to make this stuff, and I'm one of them."[239] Further, "And *even with a good lab and staff to help run it, it might take me a year* to come up with a product as good."[240]

Spertzel further stated, "The FBI spent between 12 and 18 months trying to "reverse engineer" (replicate) the anthrax in the letters sent to Messrs. Daschle and Leahy without success . . . . So why should federal investigators or the news media or the American public believe that a lone scientist would be able to do so?"[241]

The killer anthrax contained silicon, but the anthrax found in Dr. Ivins' flask did not. The FBI tried to talk its way around that chemical incongruity, by suggesting that the anthrax present in the mailings *absorbed* silicon from its surroundings. Lawrence Livermore National Laboratories refuted that theory: The silicon found in the killer anthrax was *"intentionally added to the killer anthrax."*[242] Neither Dr. Ivins, nor the research facility at Fort Detrick, possessed the capability to add silicon to anthrax.

Sandia National Lab found iron and tin in the killer anthrax— but iron and tin were not found in Ivins' flask of anthrax. Further, "Sandia also found that there was a strain of bacteria in one of the anthrax letters not present in Ivins' flask."[243]

Multiple sources have documented that the investigative case against Ivins was as non-meritorious as the scientific. Even the FBI's own handwriting analysts did not assert that Ivins wrote the handwritten note, that accompanied the anthrax letters. No textile fibers were found in Ivins' office, residence or vehicles which matched the fibers found on the scotch tape used to seal the envelopes. No pens were found which matched the ink used to address the envelopes. Further, "The FBI could not place Ivins at the crime scene [from which the anthrax mailings were sent] with evidence such as gas station or other receipts, or credit card charges, at the time the letters were mailed in September and October of 2001."[244]

As Meryl Nass, M.D., anthrax vaccine expert and professional colleague of Dr. Ivins observes, the FBI pointed out that Ivins had use of a copy machine— but the FBI failed to publicly admit that Ivins' copier was *not* the machine used to print the notes contained in the anthrax mailings. The FBI stressed that the anthrax letter envelopes were sold in Frederick, Maryland, where Fort Detrick is located— before admitting that millions of indistinguishable envelopes were manufactured, with sales in both Maryland and Virginia.

In *The 2001 Anthrax Deception, The Case for a Domestic Conspiracy,*[245] author Graeme MacQueen, traces the chronology— and the political exigencies— that drove the FBI's Anthrax "investigation." Immediately, after 9-11, the Administration was pushing for War in Iraq, and simultaneously ramming the pre-9-11 drafted Patriot Act— which helped usher in the Surveillance State in America— through Congress. At that time, it was expedient for the FBI to claim the Iraq-connected Al-Qaeda transmitted the lethal anthrax letters. Hence, the FBI originally claimed that Al-Qaeda committed the crime, with the support of Iraq.

However, the scientific community demolished the FBI's claim that Iraqi terrorists could have developed the highly weaponized, extremely complex, chemically modified anthrax spores. The scientific community concomitantly confirmed that the spores had to be produced from a United States government lab working for the military and federal intelligence agencies. It then became necessary for the FBI to dispel the notion that a government lab had been covertly commissioned to perform a black op with the anthrax. So, the FBI lasered in on the manufactured theory that a lone, mentally unstable scientific assassin, committed the crime. That lone scientific assassin fatally selected by the FBI's decisional apparatus— was Dr. Bruce Ivins.

Dr. Bruce Ivins died on July 29, 2008, as he was facing indictment on 5 counts of murder. Dr. Jeffery J. Adamovicz, former director of the bacteriology department at Fort Detrick told *The Washington Post*, "A lot of the tactics they used were designed to isolate him from his support. The FBI just continued to push his buttons." Indeed, the official finding was that Ivins had committed suicide by taking an overdose of Tylenol.

However, it is a finding not everyone accepts. No autopsy was performed. There was no suicide note. Dr. Meryl Nass notes that Ivins died under the watchful eye of the FBI:

> [The] FBI fails to provide any discussion of why no autopsy was performed, nor why, with Ivins under 24/7 surveillance from the house next door, with even his garbage being combed through, the FBI failed to notice that he overdosed and went into a coma. Nor is there any discussion of why the FBI didn't immediately identify tylenol as the overdose substance, and notify the hospital, so that a well-known antidote for tylenol toxicity could be given (N-acetyl cysteine, or alternatively glutathione). These omissions support the suggestion that Ivins' suicide was a convenience for the FBI. It enabled them to conclude the anthrax case, in the absence of evidence that would satisfy the courts.[246]

The senior scientists that worked with Dr. Ivins, did not believe he had committed the anthrax crimes. As Dr. Adamovicz told the *Washington Post*, "I really don't think he's the guy. I say to the FBI, 'Show me your evidence.'"[247]

Senator Patrick Leahy, one of the intended victims, believes people in the government know who was behind the Anthrax attacks:

> And I think there are people within our government — certainly from the source of it— who know where it came from. [Taps the table to let that settle in] And these people may not have had anything to do with it, but they certainly know where it came from.[248]

The FBI gave its consent in October 2001 for the remaining samples of the anthrax strain to be destroyed, making it more difficult to prove the identity of the perpetrators. As reported by *The New York Times* on November 9, 2001, "Last month, after consulting with the FBI, Iowa State University in Ames destroyed anthrax spores collected over more than seven decades and kept in more than 100 vials."[249] One consequence of the FBI-authorized destruction of anthrax spores, was the annihilation of evidence which could have been used to trace and pinpoint who was actually guilty of the Anthrax mailings.

With the death of Dr. Ivins, another Mueller inquiry had reached its end, if not Justice. Ivins' death could have been the result of suicide— or the result of foul play. In either case, Dr. Ivins' death was a fortuitous ending for Robert Mueller's inquiry, which spared Mueller's inquest the scrutiny inherent in a public trial.

Chapter 8

Weapons of Mass Destruction

The claim that Iraq had Weapons of Mass Destruction was of monumental significance. It helped mobilize America to go to war against one nation— Iraq— when America had been attacked on 9-11 by operatives from another nation— Saudi Arabia.

The claim that Iraq possessed Weapons of Mass Destruction helped set the political stage for a War in Iraq. In that War, which began in March 2003, over 4,500 American soldiers have been killed. At least 134,000 Iraqi civilians have died as a result of the War, according to a Study released by the Costs of War Project by Watson Institute for International Studies at Brown University in March, 2013.[250] As of 2011, 32,226 American soldiers had been wounded, as reported by the Pentagon. "Hundreds of thousands— maybe more than half a million [have been injured]" as reported by Dan Froomkin of *Huffington Post* on February 19, 2012, "if you take into account all the men and women who returned from their deployments with traumatic brain injuries, post-traumatic stress, depression, hearing loss, breathing disorders, diseases and other long-term health problems."[251] Moreover, as of March 2013, "The U.S. War in Iraq has cost $1.7 trillion with an additional $490 billion in benefits owed to war veterans, expenses that could grow to more than $6 trillion over the next four decades counting interest" according to the Watson Institute Study, as reported by *Reuters World News* on March 14, 2013.[252]

The claim that Iraq had Weapons of Mass Destruction was not only of monumental significance. It was also false. As American military leaders, international observers and government officials who had their boots on the ground in Iraq, have now affirmed, the mantra that Iraq had weapons of mass destruction, was not accurate intelligence, merely effective incitement.

General Anthony Zinni is a former Marine Corps General, and former Commander in Chief of the United States Central Command, who in 2002 was selected to be a special envoy for the United States to Israel and the Palestinian Authority. As reported by Dylan Matthews of *Vox* on July 9, 2016, "Gen. Anthony Zinni, ... [stated] in a documentary, 'In doing work with the CIA on Iraq WMD, through all the briefings I heard at Langley, I never saw one piece of credible evidence that there was an ongoing program.'"[253]

The claim that Iraq had Weapons of Mass Destruction was not only of monumental significance. It was not only false. It was also parroted by Robert Mueller in the lead up to the War on Iraq. Thus, on February 11, 2003, Robert Mueller appeared before Congress, presumably doing what he was told to do, saying what he was told to say, making the moves he was told to make, honorable or not:

> As (CIA) Director Tenet has pointed out, Secretary Powell presented evidence last week that Baghdad has failed to disarm its weapons of mass destruction, willfully attempting to evade and deceive the international community. Our particular concern is that Saddam Hussein may supply terrorists with biological, chemical, or radiological material.[254]

96

Chapter 9

The Surveillance State

Freedom is the bulwark of constitutional democracy—freedom of movement, action, speech, association, thought.

Government Surveillance, conversely, is central to government power— and inimical to freedom. Surveillance gives the government knowledge of people's movements, actions, speech, associations— and thereby their thoughts. Government knowledge of people's movements, actions, speech, associations and thoughts is a predicate to government's ability to retaliate against people for their movements, actions, speech, associations and thoughts. The government's power to retaliate against the people for their actions, words and associations, constitutes the government's power to intimidate and harm those that disagree with it, criticize it, or want to change its direction. The government's power to *retaliate* against people is, embryonically, the government's power to *control* the people's actions, words and associations. The government's power to control people, gives rise to the government's power to deprive them of freedom, render them powerless— rob them of self-determination.

Thus, Surveillance is central to government knowledge of people's speech and actions, which in turn activates the government's power to retaliate against citizens for even lawful speech and actions, which translates to government control, which constitutes the government's power to abrogate freedom, strip away people's power, deny self-determination.

Ultimately, surveillance is an instrument of government control. Surveillance is inimical to freedom. The preservation of freedom requires limits upon government surveillance on law abiding citizens. Total surveillance is predicate— to total control.

In pre-technological societies, surveillance inhered in networks of spies and informants. Technological developments have magnified the government's power to spy. Thus, in post-digital societies, with centralized, technological apparati that record, store and transmit electronic and digital communications, the government is able to monitor, record, store, use— or blackmail with— every digital or telephonic conversation in which a citizen engages. The government's ability to spy has exponentially expanded in the digital age.

Americans were told that the 9-11 terrorist attack, and a need to prevent its recurrence, justified a Surveillance State in America. As long-time CIA analyst, Ray McGovern, and former NSA technical director of world military and geopolitical analysis, William Binney, have written, "How did (data) collection go on steroids? You've heard it a thousand times— 'After 9/11 everything changed.'" [255]

The claim that 9-11 justified omnipresent monitoring is spurious. Before 9-11, many warnings were sent, red flags waved, and alarms rung, to alert senior intelligence executives, top-level federal officials, even the White House. Top officials ignored the warnings. America didn't need the capacity to spy on the digital and telephonic conversations of every American to prevent 9-11. America didn't need blanket surveillance. America simply needed senior intelligence and government officials that had the wisdom and backbone to heed the repeated alarms of the rank and file intelligence agents, the soldiers in the trenches, and citizen whistleblowers.

David Graham's Wars

One of those whistleblowers was Dr. David M. Graham, D.D.S., a Louisiana born and raised dental surgeon, decorated Vietnam veteran, investigative journalist, author of *The 9/11 Graham Report*— Keithville, Louisiana country boy.

Graham was born in 1939 and grew up in the Northwest Louisiana countryside outside Keithville. When he and his brothers enrolled in High School at C.E. Byrd in nearby Shreveport, they had the distinction of being the shortest boys in the school. He was one of about 150 kids that tried out for the High School baseball team, and didn't make the team. By the time he matriculated at Centenary College, also in Shreveport, he had grown some, his skills had improved, and he made the College baseball team as a late walk-on, helping sew his own uniform, after the team's uniforms had already been handed out to the first-tier players.

After graduating from Dental School, he enlisted and served three years in the Air Force, including two in Viet Nam. In Viet Nam, in addition to giving dental care to villagers, he gave emergency triage medical care to seriously wounded American soldiers. David Graham was awarded a Bronze Star for his service in Viet Nam, where he volunteered on 62 Med Cap missions into the Viet-Cong-infiltrated South Vietnamese countryside to provide dental care to South Vietnamese villagers, and win their allegiance to the South Vietnamese-American alliance. He never knew in advance whether the village he and his dental team entered to provide treatment, harbored the Viet Cong. Graham volunteered for every medical mission, because he was single. Some of the other men had families.

Upon his return to Shreveport after the War, he made his mark as a dentist. He preached against the use of mercury fillings, some 25 years ahead of his time. He independently studied the connection between gum disease and other pathologies of the body. He was well known in Shreveport for providing free dental service to the poor. Graham was described by Researcher Sander Hicks:

> Graham was an independent radio journalist who stood up to local political corruption. He was a Vietnam veteran who volunteered for medical missions in a combat zone. He was an evangelical Christian who clothed the poor, and a Shreveport dentist who pioneered advanced, healthy techniques.[256]

"When a homeless man moved into an old trailer on his property, Dr. David Graham didn't call the cops. He brought out hot soup and clean clothes. . . . . He struck up a conversation. In time, the homeless guy got back on his feet."[257]

Graham started several companies, including a thoroughbred horse racing business. These businesses saw both dizzying success and cataclysmic failure, with Graham becoming a millionaire several times, before losing the money, without ever developing an attachment to money. He was a radio talk show host, investigating causes near and far.

In the year 2000, Graham started a business called AdvaLife, that was predicated upon his research into the relationship between gum disease and overall health, and which marketed health products he developed. It was through his research of the physiological connections between gum disease and systemic pathologies, that he met Dr. Mohammed Habeeb Ahmed at LSU Medical Center in Shreveport, Louisiana in March 2000. It was through Dr. Ahmed and his AdvaLife business, that he met Jamal Khan in September, 2000, also in Shreveport. It was through Jamal Khan, that in October 2000, Graham met Fayez Banihammad and Nawaf al Hazmi in Shreveport.

In or about March of 2000, Graham was researching the links between gum disease and heart attacks at LSU-Medical Center in Shreveport, when he met a physician, Dr. Mohammed Ahmed. Later in 2000, Graham met one of Ahmed's friends, Jamal Khan, who represented that he wanted to invest in Graham's company, AdvaLife. Graham later met with Khan at Khan's townhouse in September of 2000, to discuss AdvaLife.

While at Kahn's Shreveport townhouse in September of 2000, Graham saw three boxes of documents on Khan's kitchen floor, bearing the names Nawaf al-Hazmi, Khalid al-Mihdhar and Fayez Banihammad. Graham wrote their names on his hand, while Khan was out of the room, to help him remember them.

About two weeks later, on October 7, 2000, Graham was again visiting Khan in his townhouse. Graham, who used local diners as his business offices, and for informal political forums over coffee, eggs and bacon, was coming to notice that Khan did not like meeting in public. At that time, Dr. Ahmed, the physician working at LSU-Medical Center, walked into Khan's townhouse with two young Saudi men, Nawaf al-Hazmi and Fayez Banihammad. Dr. Ahmed represented that the young men were Medical Doctors from

101

Chicago. "One glared at Graham, the dentist said, and the other was unable to carry on a conversation in English."[258]

Jamal Khan was averse to meeting in public. Two of the four men, Nawaf al-Hazmi and Fayez Banihammad, were posing as physicians. Barksdale U.S. Air Force Base, one of the American military's largest nuclear installations, is located across the Red River from Shreveport, in Bossier City, Louisiana. Barksdale houses the 2nd Bomb Wing, a fleet of B-52 bomber planes, and a large arsenal of nuclear bombs and weapons, designed to be dispatched by the bombers of the 2nd Bomb Wing. Somehow, Jamal Khan "had special access" to Barksdale U.S. Air Force Base.[259] It was at Barksdale Air Force Base (BAFB) "where [Jamal Khan] enjoyed dating women of the U.S. military."[260] As Graham later recounted, Khan plied women at Barksdale with gifts and jewelry. The Arabic men spoke of purchasing a van and driving it onto the Base.

Certainly, Graham's scientific education as a dental surgeon, his military training as a member of the United States Army and his disquisitive experience as a radio journalist, honed his investigative instincts. Perhaps it was his growing up a country boy outside of Keithville, Louisiana, more than anything, that prepared him for the challenges he now faced at 61 years of age. Graham, the Vietnam Veteran, pioneering dental scientist, investigative journalist— and Keithville country boy— knew something was wrong. Graham's thought at the time: these Middle Eastern men were planning to get their hands on a van, fill it with explosives, breach the Security of the nuclear installation at Barksdale Air Force Base, get onto the base and launch a terrorist attack.

Years later, David Graham still remembered the moment when he knew his fears were justified— the moment he overheard Jamal Khan tell Dr. Ahmed: "My father has recently been to meet Osama bin Laden."[261]   When Khan spoke of his father meeting with bin Laden, Graham knew it was time to act.

The appearance of Nawaf al-Hazmi and Fayez Banihammad in Shreveport, Louisiana in the fall of 2000 was not entirely a bolt out of the blue. Dr. Graham had personally met Nawaz al-Hazmi and Fayez Banihammad through Dr. Ahmed at Jamal Khan's Shreveport townhouse, in September of 2000. Graham had seen Khalid al Mihdhar's name scribed on a box on the floor of Jamal Khan's townhouse, along with boxes labeled in the names of al-Hazmi and Banihammad, when Graham was at Khan's townhouse in September of 2000.

Al-Hazmi was one of two terrorists, along with Khalid al Mihdhar, who arrived in Los Angeles by February, 2000. Saudi agent, Omar al-Bayoumi, got paid, without showing up for work, as an employee of a California firm that contracted with the Saudi Ministry of Defense and Aviation. Al-Bayoumi then worked as a handler for the two Saudi terrorists, al-Hazmi and Mihdhar. As Andrew Cockburn has reported, al-Bayoumi "invited [the two Saudis] to move to San Diego, found them an apartment, paid their first month's rent, helped them open a bank account, and introduced them to members of the local Saudi community."[262] In San Diego, al-Hazmi and al Mihdar lived with a paid FBI Informant, Abdusattar Shaikh. At some point in the fall of 2000, al-Hazmi moved on from San Diego to Shreveport.

Graham determined to go undercover on his own, pursue interaction with the Middle Easterners, find out what they were up to. He even invited the men, who were Muslims, to attend the Evangelical Church, which Graham attended in Shreveport, to build a relationship with them. And Graham resolved to report the men and their suspicious activities to the federal authorities.

In November, 2000, Graham met with an FBI Agent in his Shreveport Dental Clinic, provided him names and an hour of details, and informed the Agent of his concern that the men were plotting to make a terrorist attack on Barksdale Air Force Base. Shortly thereafter, late in 2000, a Secret Service Agent visited Graham's Clinic, and Graham also informed him of the same facts.

The FBI's response? According to a complaint filed with the Office of the Inspector General for the Department of Justice filed by Sander Hicks, "The FBI allegedly responded by passing along a death threat they allegedly received against 'who ever ratted out Jamal Khan.'"[263] Graham understood that the FBI's response was an attempt to intimidate Graham into shutting his mouth.

It was October 5, 2001, some three and a half weeks after 9-11. David Graham was sitting down for breakfast at Murrells, a local Shreveport diner, when he looked at the front page of USA TODAY. On the front page, were pictures of the 19 hijackers that had perpetrated the attacks of 9-11. As Graham surveyed the pictures he was stunned— among the men pictured were Nawaf al-Hazmi and Fayez Banihammad— the two young Arab men whom Dr. Ahmed introduced to David Graham at Khan's townhouse in September, 2000.

According to post-9-11 FBI press releases, al-Hazmi was one of the hijackers that commandeered American

Airlines Flight 77, which was reportedly flown into the West wall of the Pentagon. Banihammad was one of the hijackers that seized the United Airlines Flight 175 that was flown into the World Trade Center's South Tower. Also pictured in the USA TODAY article? Khalid al Mihdhar, whose name Graham had seen written on a box on the floor of Jamal Khan's townhouse in September of 2000. Al-Mihdhar had earlier lived in San Diego with al-Hazmi, where Al-Mihdhar and al-Hazmi were supported by the Saudis and provided lodging by a paid FBI informant. According to the FBI's releases, Al-Mihdhar was one of the hijackers that, along with al-Hazmi, had hijacked American Airlines Flight 77 and flown it into the West wall of the Pentagon.

Graham was furious. He had warned federal authorities that the men were dangerous. The feds had done nothing.

Graham wanted a record made that he had personally and repeatedly warned federal agents about the suspicious activities of these interlopers before 9-11, that the FBI had taken no action on his repeated warnings— and that there was something awry in the intelligence complex. Graham repeatedly contacted the local FBI to demand what they did with his information. By November of 2001, the local FBI stopped returning Graham's calls.

Graham started writing his account of the events. He wrote a report, "The 9-11 Graham Report," about the presence of Dr. Ahmed, Jamal Khan and the two 9-11 hijackers, al-Hazmi and Banihammad in Shreveport before 9-11; about the fact that he specifically reported both their presence in Shreveport and their suspicious activities to the FBI and a Secret Service Agent before 9-11; and about the fact that federal agencies did nothing about it. Graham put the sequence of events in writing, to furnish the FBI with reports that might work their way up the chain of command, to someone who had the power and willingness to address the malfunction.

Graham was consumed with the fact that he had reported the men and their suspicious activities to federal agencies, the feds had done nothing— and a catastrophic loss of life had resulted. As a veteran, he could not comprehend how a federal agent's oath of duty could allow him to disregard threats to the safety of Americans. It was too late to stop 9-11. It was not too late to get to the bottom of who staged it, and how they got away with it.

Graham would not let go. He would not let up.

On January 31, 2002, Graham carried a 96-page manuscript reporting what he had seen and heard, to an FBI Agent in Shreveport.

Graham continued to talk to the local FBI Agents. He openly told them he intended to publish a book about the Middle Eastern men that were in Shreveport in late 2000 and thereafter; who were reported to federal agents in November of 2000, ten months before 9-11; and who were principles to the attack of 9-11. As Graham continued to speak to the local FBI Agents, their conversations became increasingly terse. As Graham got closer to publicly releasing his work, the Agents began to admonish him not to report his experience or release his written narrative. At first the admonitions not to publish were insistent; as time went on, ominous.

In May 2002, local FBI Agent Ray Spoon went to David Graham's Dental Clinic to dissuade him from taking his report to the Congressional Joint Inquiry that was investigating 9-11. Agent Spoon asked Graham, "How's your health, Dr. Graham." Increasing the pitch and volume of his voice, rising out of his chair, Spoon then stated, "I don't think you understand, Dr. Graham, how's your health?" Graham was unintimidated.

On another occasion, Graham was met by one or more Secret Service Agents, on his way out of church.

As Sander Hicks has documented,

Moore said the FBI strongly urged Dr. Graham not to publish his book '*The 9/11 Graham Report*.'[264]

As long-time friend, Vernon Moore, told reporter Jordan Green,

"David was a headstrong person," Moore said. "And he was determined to do the book deal. And he spent a lot of time on it. And that was his life, ... It was a heck of a story. And (the FBI) told him not to. And he was going to do it regardless. But— it never got off the ground, put it that way."[265]

Graham slept with an AK-47, and a bag packed with a pistol, the essential evidence he had uncovered and a manuscript of his report.

"Initially," as Jordan Green reports, "[Graham's] report was compiled for the benefit of the FBI and other federal law enforcement agencies."[266] But after a local FBI

Agent made not-so-veiled threats against Graham, he prepared a more complete narrative of the events he experienced, to transmit to the Congressional Joint Inquiry that was examining the actions of federal intelligence agencies before and after 9-11. Graham "began reaching out to elected officials, including Louisiana (4th District) Congressman, Jim McCrery,"[267] and McCrery reportedly forwarded the report to then Georgia Congressman, Saxby Chambliss, who passed it on to Porter Goss, then Chair of the House Committee on Select Intelligence.

Graham made plans to hand deliver his report to Congress's Joint Select Committee on Intelligence ("Joint Inquiry") in Washington, that was investigating the intelligence agency failures surrounding the events of 9-11.

Shortly before his departure to Washington, someone fired shots into the home in which David Graham was living.

In June 2002, Graham made the trek to Washington to hand deliver his report, careful to take a winding trail that would make it harder for rogue federal agents to follow him, or thwart his mission. As Green reports:

> In June 2002, Graham drove to Washington, DC so he could personally deliver the report to the Joint Select Intelligence Committee ["Joint Inquiry"], which was tasked with investigating the causes of the Sept. 11, 2001 terrorist attacks. . . . . Graham reportedly made a harrowing journey to Washington, DC, zig-zagging along Interstate 20 to avoid interception, and making the final leg of the trip accompanied by [Tracy Ammons] a one-time

lobbyist for the Christian Coalition after a stop in Charleston, SC.[268]

As Graham himself write in 2002, as he took a weaving path to avoid rogue federal agents that might be trailing him, and take his findings from Louisiana to Washington, "A heretofore fearless man began to fear— his own government."[269]

In June 2002, Graham hand delivered his report to counsel for the Congressional Joint Inquiry in Washington.

Later, back in Shreveport, Graham covertly videotaped a series of far-ranging post-9-11 conversations with Dr. Ahmed and Jamal Khan, who had remained in Louisiana after 9-11, and who both admitted that al-Hazmi and Banihammad— the 9-11 hijackers— had been in Shreveport before 9-11. Graham covertly videotaped the conversations between Dr. Ahmed and himself in Graham's Clinic in June, 2002. Graham covertly videotaped the conversations between Jamal Khan and Graham in Graham's Clinic in March, 2003. In lengthy conversations, Ahmed and Kahn both acknowledged that Nawaf al-Hazmi and Fayez Banihammad had in fact been in Shreveport before 9-11. As Jamal Khan stated in a covertly videotaped conversation, "Those people is gone. What happened September eleventh happened."[270]

Graham delivered a copy of one of the videotapes to a member of Congress.

When federal agents responded to his persistent reports with hostility, and when the Congressional Joint Inquiry into 9-11 provided no concrete response to his first hand, pre-9-11 observations of the hijackers in Shreveport, Louisiana,

Graham perfected his report and transformed it into a book, *The 9/11 Graham Report*, to report what he saw and heard, to the Court of last resort— the American people. As Green reports, "When elected officials appeared to neglect the report, Graham decided to present it to an audience of last resort: the American people."[271]

"In the last weeks of May [2004], [Shreveport Private Investigator Rick] Turner recalled [that] Graham called him and said, "I need another ten copies of those [video] tapes [of conversations with Jamal Khan and Dr. Ahmed] . . . . Things are heating up."[272]

On the Memorial Day weekend of 2004, Graham went to Houston to see his close friend, Gordon Klausman, and speak one last time with Klausman's wife, who was in the hospital dying of cancer. That weekend, Graham was on the verge of publishing the report that had grown into a book, The *9/11 Graham Report*. Before he went to Houston to see Gordon Klausman and his wife, Graham left a copy of his manuscript with a close friend in Shreveport, Richard Wilkes. He also left an instruction: he might have one last paragraph to add to his book. As both Graham and the FBI knew, Graham was on the verge of publishing his book.

On the night of May 28, 2004, a subdued Graham joined Klausman's friend, Ronald K. Smith, for drinks at the Upper Deck on Lake Conroe, near Houston. Klausman's friend, Smith, was a retired auxiliary member of the Coast Guard. The Coast Guard had recently been subsumed within the Department of Homeland Security.

On the night of May 28, 2004, as David Graham was close to finalizing and publishing his book, *The 9-11 Graham Report*, Graham was poisoned, apparently when someone dropped antifreeze in his drink at the Upper Deck at Lake Conroe, Texas.

Lufkin, Texas is approximately equidistant between Houston and Shreveport. The most severe effects of the poisoning occurred the next day about noon, as Graham was driving back from Houston to Shreveport, and Graham was stricken while in the Lufkin, Texas area. Suffering from seizures and multi-organ shutdown, Graham was transported to the ER in Lufkin, Texas, fighting for his life, and placed in intensive care at the Lufkin Hospital. His son states that the Doctors in Lufkin saved his life by administering an IV of Everclear.

Antifreeze is a sweet tasting, but highly toxic substance. Medical texts confirm that the most toxic effects of antifreeze poisoning do not manifest immediately, but around 12 hours after ingestion of the poison, after the body metabolizes the chemicals present in antifreeze, and converts them into more lethal toxins. Graham was stricken around noon on May 29, 2004, as he drove in the Lufkin area— roughly 12 hours after his drinks at the Upper Deck in Lake Conroe the night of May 28, 2004.

Sources close to Graham state that after Graham was hospitalized at Lufkin, the FBI told the Lufkin doctors that Graham was "crazy" and "suicidal"[273]— in essence, he did not deserve medical treatment.

Within two days of admission, Graham was transferred by helicopter to Hermann Hospital in Houston for advanced care. At Herrman Hospital, while immediate family wrestled with the decision of whether or not to remove David Graham from life support, FBI Agents materialized, and tried to discourage the doctors from saving his life, again telling

Graham's doctors that Graham was "crazy" and "suicidal."[274] Implicitly, the FBI Agents were telling the Houston physicians, Graham did not deserve their best medical efforts. Graham's son Davey later recalled that his father's cardiologist came in "screaming to the nurses about how he doesn't think it's right that he's spending so much time on this guy that the FBI thinks is just nuts."[275]

One of the doctors in Houston tacitly encouraged the family to consider pulling Graham off life support, telling them that his chances of survival were 1%. Still later, one of the doctors told them, Graham's chances were much less than that, that he was walking, alone, in a very deep and snow laden forest, with no way to find his way back home.

Within two days of his poisoning, a local FBI Agent stated to one Shreveporter, that David Graham was dead. Staff at David Graham's Dental Clinic told patients and concerned friends the same thing, that David Graham was dead. His Clinic Staff's subsequent explanation for making this false statement, morphed between the justification that the FBI *told* them that David Graham was dead, to the explication that the FBI told them *to say* David Graham was dead

Back in Shreveport, the FBI wasted no time in not only discrediting Graham, but in pointing the finger away from the FBI for the circumstances surrounding Dr. Graham's death. Thus, the FBI suggested to the local media almost immediately after his poisoning, that Dr. Graham may have been suicidal and attempted to take his own life, because of business or personal reversals

Thus, the local ABC affiliate reported that "Federal authorities in Shreveport said they are not involved and don't

112

know if there is anything sinister to Graham's illness or if it was a suicide attempt or was connected to Graham's personal or business life."[276]   The local ABC Reporter who covered the story, later said that "it was his FBI source in Shreveport, not he, who introduced the notion of suicide."[277]

Graham's friends never bought the suicide narrative floated by the Feds. Graham was courageous, upbeat, on a mission for which he deemed it worthy to risk his life. The entire notion of suicide was antithetical to who he was, what he believed, his belief in the cause he fought for. And it was diametrically opposed to his character. David Graham had volunteered for 62 Med Cap missions into enemy-infested territory in Viet Nam, choosing to embark on every Med Cap mission that was offered by his command.

The FBI-spun tale that David Graham had tried to commit suicide, was another 9-11 cover story— self-serving and false.

Someone had attempted to kill David Graham the night of May 28, 2004 at the Upper Deck, by pouring antifreeze into his drink. Graham survived the poisoning attempt. He survived due in part to the efforts of medical staff in Lufkin and Houston, that would not be dissuaded from their medical mission by the FBI.

And, as Graham would often later brag, he had come out of a coma with no brain damage. He had come out of the attempt on his life with his mental faculties intact. But because of the neurotoxic effect of the antifreeze, he would never again lift himself out of a bed. Never again walk. And he suffered a type of functional paralysis of his voice box— after that day he could speak only in a grating rasp, struggling to speak and be heard.

After Graham was poisoned, the FBI interviewed David's good friend, Gordon Klausman— whose wife David had gone to see one last time, before she succumbed to cancer. The federal agents asked not one question about David Graham being poisoned. Instead, they focused their questions on what David Graham knew about 9-11. As Sander Hicks has documented, "When Gordon Klausman went to do an interview with the Houston FBI, he noted that they weren't curious about the circumstances of Graham's poisoning. They were interested more in what Graham had been researching, the 9/11 hijackers."[278]

As reported by Jordan Green:

> Shortly after Graham's sudden illness, Klausman was interviewed by the Houston FBI. He was surprised when the agent peppered him with questions about Graham's 9-11 research.

> "I found that very strange," Klausman said. "I was expecting, 'What happened to him? What he did that night, what might have been the possibility of him ingesting some substance?"[279]

Graham died on September 17, 2006, lying in a Nursing Home bed in Shreveport, at the age of 67, over two years and four months after he was poisoned, and over five years after the catastrophic event that his warnings, if heeded, could have prevented.

Graham was eulogized as a patriot at his memorial service in September 2006:

If only he had consented to keep silent before 9-11, not to report the suspicious men, it would have been better for him, but worse for the nation . . . . If only he had consented to keep his mouth closed after 9-11, it would have been better for him but worse for the nation. If only he hadn't written a book about his investigation, it would have been better for him, but worse for the nation. David fought with the recognition of consequences. He knew, and he mentioned to others, that what he was doing someday might get him hurt or worse. He understood the consequences. But he also understood the consequences of saying nothing and remaining silent in a republic, a constitutional democracy that values truth and honors freedom.[280]

"In the wake of his (Dr. Graham's) death," the FBI falsely denied that it had met with Dr. Graham before 9-11.[281] Thus, "Former Special Agent Ray Spoon told the local media that Graham had not met with the FBI before 9/11."[282] But Sander Hicks went directly to the FBI Office in Shreveport in October 2007, and spoke to an FBI Agent that told the truth: FBI Agents had met with Dr. Graham before 9-11: "(T)hat day in the FBI's tiny white lobby, agent Steve Hayes admitted that he had in fact met with Graham before the attacks."[283] As Hicks observes, "Hayes admitted to us that yes, he had met with Dr. Graham before 9/11."[284]

Hicks had personally gone to question local FBI Agents at their Shreveport office in October of 2007, about Graham's 2006 death. In 2007, "The Shreveport FBI office [experienced] a high rate of turnover."[285] Thus, the Special Agent in Charge transferred out of Shreveport in 2007.

115

"Agent Ray Spoon, a key player in the Graham case, took early retirement from FBI [around June of 2007]."[286]

Jamal Khan was the ostensible handler, at least in Shreveport, Louisiana, for 9-11 hijackers Nawaf al-Hazmi and Fayez Banihammad, and possibly Khalid al-Mihdhar. According to Hicks, one of the local FBI Agents intimated that Jamal Khan— who helped facilitate the 9-11 attack on America— was also an FBI informant. Thus, a local FBI Agent "indicated that Mohammad Jamal Khan may have in fact been the FBI's informant."[287]

In a covertly recorded videotape of Jamal Khan made by Graham in 2003, Khan explains why he wasn't concerned about prosecution for having two wives— one in Pakistan and one in Texas. On the video, Khan laughs and tells Graham, "FBI— they tried to convict me of that, but they had no chance because I have a lot of people back up in Washington."[288] As Khan elaborates, "If something comes up, political friends, American friends, my ambassador there."[289] As Jordan Green notes, "In the videotape, Khan says that he comes from an important family in Pakistan that owns farms and factories."[290]

Jordan Green reports that Khan's visa expired in 1998— over 2 years before 9-11; Khan was arrested in East Texas in October 2001 for possession of a firearm by a prohibited person, since his visa had already expired; in February 2002, he was indicted for structuring a financial transaction to evade reporting requirements, when he wired $9,999 to Pakistan. In April, 2002, Khan pled guilty with the express agreement that he could later be charged for his involvement in 9-11. As the plea agreement written by the Department of Justice (DOJ) read, *"In no case does the [government] agree that there will be no prosecution of the*

116

defendant for any crimes concerning the hijacking of any airline or any attack on any building or deaths that occurred on or about September 11, 2001."[291] The FBI knew that Jamal Khan was involved in the attack of 9-11. That much was clear in the DOJ plea agreement which explicitly reserved the right to charge Khan in connection with 9-11.

In April 2002, Khan was fined $100, sentenced to time served— and released.[292]

David Graham was a patriot and decorated military veteran who reported a legitimate threat to America, and then demanded an accounting from federal agencies for their failure to heed his explicit warnings and protect American lives.

When David Graham emerged from a coma in June, 2004, after being poisoned on May 28, 2004, he told his former employee, LeeAnne Scruggs, that he believed the FBI was guilty of poisoning him. As Jordan Green has reported, "Graham told Scruggs that he believed the FBI poisoned him."[293] Thus, Green notes, "Asked who was responsible for her boss' poisoning, Scruggs said, 'According to Dr. Graham, the FBI.'"[294]

States Sander Hicks, "Graham died a mysterious death that was never investigated. The Shreveport FBI agents were extremely hostile when I asked them why."[295] As Hicks reports,

> Moore said the FBI strongly urged Dr. Graham not to publish his book '*The 9/11 Graham Report.*' But Graham forged ahead. Shortly thereafter, he was poisoned. Moore told us 'For

117

some reason the US government was covering for them people . . . ."[296]

David Graham, the Patriot and decorated veteran, received very different treatment, than Jamal Khan, the well-connected Pakistani hustler, FBI informant and handler of 9-11 hijackers. Jamal Khan was protected. David Graham was poisoned.

The FBI had stonewalled David Graham's pre-9-11 warnings in November, 2000, about the suspicious Nawaf al-Hazmi and Fayez Banihammad. The FBI had threatened him against publishing his first-hand knowledge. The FBI had tried to dissuade Doctors from rendering him life-saving treatment. The FBI had lied at the time of the poisoning, while Graham was barely clinging to life and his family was deciding whether or not to disconnect him from life support, and told Shreveporters that he was dead. The FBI suggested to the local media he may have committed suicide. The FBI falsely denied that Graham had met with them before 9-11. The FBI refused to investigate his poisoning, even as they tried to pry out of his personal friend, Gordon Klausman, anything and everything that David Graham had uncovered about the events of 9-11. The local FBI in Shreveport grew hostile when asked why they didn't investigate his poisoning. It was the FBI, David believed, who were behind his poisoning.

Mueller was FBI Director when David Graham began his vociferous post 9-11 complaints that federal agents had ignored his pre-9-11 warnings about the Saudis in Shreveport. Mueller was FBI Director when FBI Agents tried to threaten Graham out of releasing his findings. Mueller was FBI Director when David Graham was poisoned. Mueller was FBI Director when FBI Agents tried to dissuade Graham's

118

doctors from saving his life; when FBI Agents falsely reported that David Graham was dead; when FBI Agents publicly intimated that David Graham attempted suicide; when FBI Agents falsely denied that Graham had spoken to them before 9-11; when FBI agents questioned Graham's friend Gordon Klausman, not about David's death, but about how much Graham knew about 9-11; when the FBI refused to investigate Graham's poisoning; when the FBI became hostile when asked why they refused to investigate his poisoning.

At the time he was poisoned, David Graham was working to expose the pre-9-11 presence of 9-11 hijackers in Shreveport, Louisiana; the fact that their suspicious activities were duly— and repeatedly— reported to federal authorities; the fact that the feds did nothing to detain or stop them; the fact that the individuals reported were later involved in the largest terrorist attack on American soil in history; the fact that, if they had been questioned— 9-11 could have been prevented.

David Graham was also poisoned in the wake of Mueller's efforts to misrepresent to the American people that the United States government received no warnings before 9-11, and in the midst of Mueller's ongoing efforts to conceal the role of the Saudi Government in 9-11.

Which raises the question: Was Dr. David M. Graham another victim of the Mueller method?

9-11 Coverup

Prior to 9-11, Federal Intelligence Agencies received reports that: Al Qaeda terrorists Nawaf al-Hazmi and Khalid al-Mihdhar, were directly or indirectly connected to radical

119

Muslim Cleric Fahad al-Thumairy in America, through their handler, al-Bayoumi; al-Hazmi and al-Mihdhar were tenants of a paid FBI informant in San Diego, and were being supported by Saudi officials; Saudis were laundering money in and into America; immigrants from Middle Eastern Nations were taking flying lessons across America; suspicious Middle Easterners, were present in Shreveport, Louisiana, posing as physicians, talking about breaching one of America's top nuclear installations across the Red River at Barksdale Air Force Base, with at least one of the their number linked to Osama bin Laden. The CIA knew that Al-Hazmi and al-Mihdhar were Al Qaeda operatives and were en route to America, before they arrived in Los Angeles in early 2000.

If the FBI Directorate had responded to these, and scores of other documented reports, of suspicious activity, the 9-11 conspiracy could have been stopped in its tracks by a competent law enforcement response of investigation and interrogation. It didn't require mass surveillance of innocent citizens to stop 9-11, because a competent law enforcement response to documented reports of suspicious activities, could have stopped the conspiracy in its tracks.

9-11 also didn't require mass surveillance because of the ground-breaking work led by former National Security Agency (NSA) Technical Director of World Military and Geopolitical Analysis, William Binney. As reported by Barbara Boyd, "Binney and his collaborators demonstrated that under his program, ThinThread, all of the information necessary to stop the 9/11 hijackers was recorded by the NSA and readily available to investigators"[297]— and that information did not include, nor require, mass data collection on every American citizen.

Finally, 9-11 didn't require mass surveillance because of the avalanche of pre-9-11 intelligence warnings that came in the years, months, weeks and days leading up to the attack.

In short, a Surveillance State was not needed to prevent 9-11. 9-11 could have been prevented if top ranking officials and bureaucrats had listened to the avalanche of warnings from field agents, military officers— and ordinary citizens. It is not the rank and file federal agents or soldiers in the trenches that failed America— it was the intelligence bureaucracy and federal officialdom.

Surveillance may constitute an assault on individual freedom and civil liberties— a dangerous predicate to government control. And the events of 9-11 were a spurious pretext for the creation of a Surveillance State in America. Ironically, the failure of the intelligence establishment to effectively keep tabs on foreign criminals, has now become the pretext for the intelligence establishment to spy on every law-abiding citizen in America.

On the night of March 10, 2004, the White House Counsel and the Chief of Staff for President George W. Bush, traveled to the Washington D.C. Hospital room of Attorney General, John Ashcroft, to obtain his written authorization for the continuation of a domestic spying program the Justice Department had just determined was illegal. According to subsequent Senate testimony by James Comey, Comey and Robert Mueller rushed to Attorney General Ashcroft's bed side to stand off President Bush's subordinates, and support Ashcroft's refusal to extend the spying regimen.

Mueller supporters point to this incident, to portray Mueller as an opponent of ubiquitous eavesdropping, the defender of a constitutionally-protected, penumbra of privacy. Researchers tell a different story.

In the first instance, it is unclear whether Comey and Mueller's role in the hospital room incident was motivated by a love of constitutional rights— or a personal turf war. As reported by Dan Eggen and Paul Kane of the *Washington Post*, "'I was very angry,' Comey testified (to the Senate), 'I thought I just witnessed an effort to take advantage of a very sick man, who did not have the powers of the attorney general because *they had been transferred to me*.'"[298]

In the second instance, Mueller is hard wired into the effort to create and perpetuate a Surveillance State in America. Mueller helped preside over the construction of one of the most comprehensive surveillance networks in world history, located on American soil. Far from opposing the erection of the surveillance state, Mueller helped create, defend and expand it. Mueller gave false testimony to Congress to get approval for mass surveillance on citizens; gave false testimony to Congress to keep mass surveillance; issued Agency orders to perpetuate mass surveillance; lobbied to even expand it; violated the law to enable it; allowed federal agents to break the law with impunity to implement it— and threatened, and retaliated against, those who opposed it.

America's surveillance state is a treacherous— even treasonous— assault on Civil Liberties, and a growing menace which portends even greater damage in the future to the freedom which defines our Republic. And Robert Mueller has his fingerprints all over the efforts to enshrine a Surveillance State in America. As Barbara Boyd has observed, Mueller played "a major role in the creation of the post-9/11 surveillance state which has eviscerated and destroyed the Fourth Amendment and the rest of our Constitution's Bill of Rights."[299]

As James Bovard noted on January 29, 2018, in an editorial for *The Hill*, entitled "Robert Mueller's forgotten surveillance crime spree," "during his 11 years as director of the Federal Bureau of Investigation, Mueller's agency routinely violated federal law and the Bill of Rights."[300]

In the immediate wake of 9-11, Mueller, as newly appointed Director of the FBI, made false statements to help garner public support for an unprecedented government surveillance regime in America. Thus, Mueller stated on September 14, 2001, that "The fact that there were a number of individuals that happened to have received training at flight schools here is news, quite obviously. If we had understood that to be the case, we would have — perhaps one could have averted this."[301] Three days later, on September 17, 2001 Mueller proclaimed, "There were no warning signs that I'm aware of that would indicate this type of (pre-9-11 terrorist) operation in the country."[302] In short, Mueller misrepresented that government intelligence officials had no forewarning of the 9-11 attack, and there was nothing those officials could have done to stop the 9-11 attack.

In fact, federal intelligence agents, military officers, ordinary citizens and foreign intelligence agencies had sent a deluge of pre-9-11 warnings to top intelligence and government officials in America. Moreover, as Bovard notes, "FBI agents in Phoenix and Minneapolis had warned FBI headquarters of suspicious Arabs in flight training programs prior to 9/11."[303] Mueller's statement that the intelligence agencies had no prior warnings of foreigners learning to fly in American Flight Schools, and no advance notice of pre-9-11 preparation by Arabs on American soil, was a lie.

And that lie had a purpose: Convincing America that we needed a domestic spying apparatus, big enough to spy on all Americans, in order to protect us from foreign terrorists. As Bovard notes, "Deceit helped capture those intrusive new prerogatives."[304] Ultimately, Mueller's "protestations helped the Bush administration railroad the Patriot Act through Congress, vastly expanding the FBI's prerogatives to vacuum up Americans' personal information."[305]

Mueller's mendacity helped usher in a New Age of Surveillance in American History. The National Security Agency (NSA) secretly initiated a warrantless surveillance system called Stellar Wind after 9-11, without Congressional approval, which authorized the NSA, without specific Court Order, to collect data on the e-mails, Internet usage, texts, faxes, phone calls and financial transactions of American citizens. Under the Stellar Wind Program, this data could be collected from citizens, even though they were not indicted, accused or even suspected of illegal activity. In 2012, former top-ranking NSA analyst, William Binney, revealed that the NSA used "secure" rooms at AT&T and Verizon to tap into the major switches and satellites of those communications companies, and capture data on the digital and telephonic communications of American citizens.

As Binney and former CIA Analyst Ray McGovern revealed in *Consortiumnews.com* in May of 2018, the NSA collects and stores data concerning these e-mail and telephonic conversations, and Internet searches: "The National Security Agency (NSA) collects everything: all email, telephone calls, texts, faxes— everything, and stores it in giant databases. . . . . (T)he technical capability is available, and the policy is to 'collect it all.' All is collected and stored in vast warehouses."[306] Thus, as Binney and

McGovern note, under the Stellar Wind Program, "the NSA has been collecting and storing domestic data on virtually all U.S. citizens."[307]

The surveillance leviathan grows darker and more menacing with time. Thus, on December 15, 2016, Director of National Intelligence, James Clapper, executed authorizations to allow the NSA to give the intercepted data on citizens to all federal intelligence agencies.

While Americans' constitutional rights are violated on an epic scale by the Stellar Wind program, they are also being transgressed under the Patriot Act. As Bovard writes, "Section 215 of the Patriot Act . . . entitles the FBI to demand 'business records' that are 'relevant' to a terrorism or espionage investigation."[308] That provision was broadened by a 2006 Bush administration decree, carried out by Mueller, that directed that the telephone records of all Americans were "relevant" to terrorism investigations. Moreover, as Bovard has documented, under the Patriot Act, the number of National Security Letters (NSLs) issued by the FBI to citizens and private entities and businesses, has exploded a hundred fold.[309] NSLs entitle the FBI to seize personal records revealing "where a person makes and spends money, with whom he lives and lived before, how much he gambles, what he buys online, what he pawns and borrows, where he travels, how he invests, what he searches for and reads on the Web, and who telephones or e-mails him at home and at work."[310] As Bovard notes, the 4th Amendment notwithstanding, "The FBI can lasso thousands of people's records with a single NSL [National Security Letter]."[311]

Federal Judge Victor Marrero has declared that the FBI's issuance of NSLs under the Patriot Act is "the legislative equivalent of breaking and entering, with an ominous free pass to the hijacking of constitutional values."[312] Federal Judge Richard Leon has characterized the NSA's record collection on virtually all American citizens as "almost Orwellian," stating that he could not "imagine a more indiscriminate and arbitrary invasion than this systematic and high-tech collection and retention of personal data on virtually every single citizen for purposes of querying and analyzing it without prior judicial approval."[313] Stated former U.S. Representative John Conyers of Michigan, then ranking Democrat on the House Judiciary Committee, on June 13, 2013, Section 215 of the Patriot Act "is being used to engage in a nationwide dragnet of telecommunications records."[314] Concluded Congressman Conyers, "It's my fear that we are on the verge of becoming a surveillance state, collecting billions of electronic records on law-abiding Americans every single day."[315]

Mueller lied to help the Surveillance State gain approval by Congress and the American people. He continues to misrepresent the facts to keep it in place. Mueller was asked in a Senate Hearing in April 2005, whether the NSA can spy on the American people. Mueller answered under oath, before the U.S. Senate, "I would say generally, they are not allowed to spy or to gather information on American citizens."[316] Mueller denied that the NSA was allowed to spy and gather information on American citizens, even though at that time, Mueller and the FBI had been participating with the NSA in Stellar Wind's warrantless surveillance of citizens' emails, telephone calls, texts, faxes, financial transactions and Internet use, for over three years. As Bovard notes, Mueller's FBI engaged in further deception: "The FBI greatly understated the number of NSLs it was issuing and denied that abuses had occurred,"[317] helping pave the way for Congress to reauthorize the Patriot Act in 2006.

126

In addition to testifying falsely before Congress, Mueller advanced the surveillance agenda in other illicit ways. Though federal law was bent, and the Constitution shredded to accommodate the government's non-stop spying on American citizens, the FBI, under Mueller, reportedly violated even the exiguous laws still on the books. Thus, as Bovard reports, in 2007, "an Inspector General report revealed that FBI agents may have recklessly issued thousands of illegal"[318] National Security Letters seizing personal records. As Bovard further notes, the Electronic Freedom Foundation won public records lawsuits to obtain reports transmitted by the FBI to an Oversight Board. After reviewing the FBI reports submitted to its Oversight Board, the Foundation "concluded that the FBI may have committed 'tens of thousands' of violations of federal law, regulations or Executive Orders between 2001 and 2008."[319]

Mueller effectively allowed FBI Agents to break the law with impunity. Instead of arresting or charging FBI Agents who violated federal law, Mueller created a new federal agency. As Bovard wrote, "Rather than arresting FBI agents who broke the law, Mueller created a new FBI Office of Integrity and Compliance."[320]

Mueller began using the patently anti-constitutional Stellar Wind spying program in late 2001. Along the way, he serially issued orders to enforce the government's power to shake telephone companies down for the data on citizens' phone calls. As Bovard documents, "Several times a year, Mueller signed orders to the Foreign Intelligence Surveillance Court, swaying it to continually renew its order compelling telephone companies to deliver all their calling records (including time, duration and location of calls) to the National Security Agency."[321] As if the Surveillance Apparatus he helped build, justify and maneuver through

Congress was not oppressive enough, Mueller told the Senate Judiciary Committee on June 19, 2013 that the federal government needed even broader surveillance powers to "keep America safe."[322]

Apparently it was still not enough that, in his efforts to erect a Surveillance State on American soil, Mueller lied to Congress about the existence and substance of the federal government's spying programs; misled Congress about the supposed need for them; violated the Constitution; utilized a secret spying program, Stellar Wind, that was neither authorized by, or contemporaneously disclosed to, Congress; allowed the agency he led to break federal law with impunity; issued orders to the FISA Court asking them to rubberstamp the data mining of law abiding citizens; and urged Congress to increase the Government's power to spy on its own citizens.

Mueller also retaliated against those who questioned the righteousness and efficacy of a federal mass surveillance regime. Long-time NSA Official and surveillance expert, William Binney proved that a ubiquitous surveillance dragnet of the citizenry was not necessary to prevent 9-11; a surgical, digital approach, would have protected America from both terrorists— and privacy-obliterating government overreach.[323] Mueller's FBI retaliated against Binney and his colleagues for having the audacity to demonstrate the truth— pervasive surveillance of the American people was not necessary to prevent 9-11:

> Binney and his collaborators demonstrated that under his program, ThinThread, all of the information necessary to stop the 9/11 hijackers was recorded by the NSA and readily available to investigators. For that, Robert Mueller sent

the FBI to raid and harass Binney and his collaborators, bringing criminal charges against one of them, Thomas Drake, which were later dropped.[324]

As Mueller prepared to exit Stage Right from his role as FBI Director in June of 2013, Mueller's parting shots included more false testimony to Congress, more eleventh-hour efforts to advance the surveillance agenda. On June 13, 2013, Mueller told the House Judiciary Committee, that if the massive surveillance regime had been in place before 9-11, the attack could have been prevented. Because the surveillance regime was not in place, there was not an opportunity to "derail" the plot: "If we had had this program in place at the time," Mueller testified, there would have been an ability to locate a key conspirator by tracing a phone number; there would have been an opportunity to conduct *Investigation, Interrogation* and *Detention*; and Agents could have "derailed the plan."[325]   As Mueller testified before the House Judiciary Committee on June 13, 2013:

> One last point. The 9/11 Commission, itself, indicated that *investigations* or *interrogations* of al-Mihdhar, once he was identified, could have yielded evidence of connections to other participants in the 9/11 plot. The simple fact of their *detention* could have derailed the plan. In any case, the opportunity was not there. If we had had this program that opportunity would have been there.[326]

Furthermore, Mueller continued, "If we had this program, that opportunity would have been there."[327]

Because the surveillance program was not in place, "the opportunity was not there."[328]

What Mueller did *not* tell the House Judiciary Committee was arguably more important than what he did tell the Committee. Namely, the opportunity to "derail" the plan *was* there: An avalanche of intel, flashing lights, red flags, ringing bells, resounding alarms— including the documented reports by federal agents that Arab immigrants were training in Flight Schools across America, without any apparent connection to professional or career objectives. Mueller didn't tell the House Committee about the pre-9-11 warnings and reports that came from field agents, military personnel, citizens, intelligence assets, foreign intelligence agencies; that top intelligence and Government Officials ignored the warnings— or intentionally buried them. Mueller did not tell the House Committee that a paid FBI informant, al-Bayoumi, entertained and helped lodge and acclimate several Muslim terrorists in San Diego well before 9-11; that these men were being given lodging by a paid FBI informant in San Diego, *after* they were already identified as terrorists by the CIA. Mueller did not tell the House Committee that these terrorists, given cover in San Diego, included Khalid Al-Mihdhar— the very hijacker whom Mueller said could have been questioned, and whose inside knowledge could have been used to "derail" 9-11.

And Mueller didn't tell Congress that if FBI Agents in Louisiana or Washington had listened to the reports of highly suspicious persons and activities by a decorated Viet Nam veteran, David Graham, before 9-11, federal agents could have conducted *Investigation, Interrogation* and *Detention* of the two terrorists and "derailed the plan." In short, Mueller didn't tell Congress that the FBI could have prevented 9-11 simply by following up on David Graham's lead, and

130

adhering to the law enforcement formula outlined by Mueller himself before Congress on June 13, 2013: *Investigation, Interrogation* and *Detention*. Mueller didn't tell Congress that, because of bureaucratic blunders or worse, the FBI bureaucracy failed to order *Investigation, Interrogation* and *Detention* before 9-11 with respect to known terrorists and highly suspicious activities.

What Mueller didn't tell the House Committee, ultimately, was that 9-11 could have been "derailed"— if the decision-makers were paying attention or had wanted to stop it.

Benjamin Franklin famously stated, "Those who would give up essential Liberty, to purchase a little temporary Safety, deserve neither Liberty nor Safety." This maxim signifies, at least in part, that those that demand that we sacrifice liberty in order to gain security, are often statist wolves in sheep's clothing— while they want us to surrender our liberty, they have no intention of providing security.

Mueller has insisted that over 320 million Americans hand over a vital part of their freedoms— ostensibly in trade for security. He's arguably not done enough to provide security— and live up to his end of the Faustian bargain. Thus, Mueller's entire leitmotiv— at least his recurring political chorus— is that America needs a Surveillance State because it produces sound investigation of terrorism, which in turn secures safety.

While Mueller's words tout the value of sound investigation, his actions express the opposite sentiment. Thus, Mueller and the FBI helped whisk the bin Ladens, Saudi Royalty and their retinue out of America within days of 9-11, forever foreclosing meaningful interrogation of persons prominently at interest— actions which Chris Farrell of Judicial Watch deems a "disgraceful failure."[329]   Mueller lied and told America that there were no pre-9-11 warnings. In fact, Federal agents made manifold reports about the suspicious pre-911 activities of the hijackers, and about the network of support provided the hijackers directly and indirectly by the Saudi Government.

Instead of following up on pre-9-11 leads, Mueller tried to conceal them. He tried to stop the Joint Commission from investigating the fact that an FBI informant in San Diego hosted two hijackers; tried to stop the Joint Commission from discovering that Saudi officials and their contacts provided these two hijackers with money, resources and lodging. Mueller used his authority to block the release of classified documents which would have exposed Saudi involvement, and incompetence or worse at the highest levels of American government. Mueller shut down interrogations that could have rendered relevant evidence— while he ordered the detention and abuse of misfortunate foreigners, "dragnetted" off the streets of New York, who had no culpability in the events of 9-11.

In short, with respect to 9-11, Mueller has not *conducted* an investigation, so much as he has *obstructed* an investigation. His efforts betray more of an effort to *conceal* the culpability of the perpetrators— than to *reveal* their culpability. With respect to the attack of 9-11, he has not labored to uncover the truth. He has striven to cover it up. It is difficult to rationally look at his actions and avoid the conclusion that his real motive for constructing a Surveillance State is not to investigate and expose terrorists— but to spy on Americans.

Mueller has indicated that he is concerned about the Civil Liberties of Americans. As he testified on June 13, 2013 before the House Judiciary Committee, "The challenge in a position such as I have held in the last 11 years is to balance on the one hand the security of the nation and on the other hand the civil liberties that we enjoy in this country."[330] Mueller's assertion that he's concerned about the Civil Liberties of Americans may be the biggest lie of all. Mueller was awash in the massive, warrantless surveillance of the emails, Internet searches, telephone calls, texts, faxes and financial transactions of hundreds of millions of law-abiding Americans. While he was immersed in anti-constitutional programs, Mueller lied about them to Congress as often as could, advanced them as effectively as he could, denied their existence as well as he could. Mueller's professed concern about "security?" His actions in covering for the true culprits of 9-11, shatters any illusion that Mueller's focus is security.

Mueller implicitly argues that the perpetual and ubiquitous data collection of the digital and telephonic communications of millions of law-abiding Americans— is constitutional. Mueller's feeble effort to argue that the Surveillance State is constitutional, continually resorts to a single Supreme Court case, and the tracing of a single phone call— to a single robber. As Marcy Wheeler has written,

> The US Supreme Court has held that phone metadata is not protected by the fourth amendment, Mueller [has] said repeatedly. He was referring to a 1979 Supreme Court case, Smith v. Maryland, which held that people did not have a reasonable expectation of privacy regarding the numbers they call, because they willingly give up those numbers to the company to connect their call.

And so, because the Supreme Court approved the collection of one robber's phone records in 1979, Mueller insisted it meant it was reasonable for FBI and NSA to collect and aggregate the phone records for every American today and forever.[331]

Chapter 10

The War on Donald Trump

Whitey Bulger, the Pan Am bombing, BCCI, Ruby Ridge, the 9-11 Investigation, Anthrax, Weapons of Mass Destruction, the Surveillance State— Mueller's career may be described by an astonishing, even dizzying, chronicle of cover-ups, corruption and collusion. From a historical perspective, it is perhaps symmetrical— from Mueller's perspective possibly preordained— that now, at the apex of his career, Mueller is at the pinnacle of his political potency and destructive potential. After decades of striving to accomplish Deep State objectives and Police State agendas, Mueller is poised— he thinks— to topple the Presidency. And he is using the well-honed techniques of deceit and treachery that he has employed for decades to victimize the innocent and protect the guilty.

Jerome Corsi has masterfully described the Deep State plot to get rid of President Trump in his book, *Killing the Deep State, The Fight to Save President Trump.* As Corsi documents, the Deep State War on Donald Trump began before Mueller was appointed as Special Counsel on May 17, 2017. In fact, Corsi points out, the Deep State declared War on Donald Trump before November 8, 2016, when Trump was elected.[332]

Corsi argues that Trump was targeted by the Deep State because he threatened the cash-driven political schemes of international financiers and their accomplices in national governments across the Globe: the Deep State's operation of "the international drug trade while supporting the military-industrial complex in a policy of perpetual war;"[333] "2009-

135

like government bailouts . . . to keep from exploding the multi-trillion-dollar fiat currency debt bubble;"[334] the continued printing of fiat currency by central bankers to "continue funding perpetual military conflicts;"[335] "the expansion of international trade deals [favorable to multinational corporations] . . . that would undercut the US [with] readily available cheap labor to government-subsidized commercial operations [in foreign countries];"[336] "continued open borders and a massive influx of Middle Eastern refugees as the US rushed"[337] to extinction as a sovereign Nation.

Thus, Trump was a threat to the military, political and economic machinations of global operators. According to Corsi, he was also a threat to expose the betrayals of national interest by former administrations:

> The risk the Deep State faced if Trump actually succeeded in winning the election was the exposure of four traitorous US presidencies. George H. W. Bush, along with Bill Clinton, George W. Bush and Barack Obama, engineered such criminal travesties as the invasion of Iraq, a "fast-and-furious" gunrunning to the Mexican drug cartels, more illegal gunrunning to Libya and Syria, as well as a plan to support the Muslim Brotherhood's penetration of the top levels of the US national security apparatus . . . .[338]

President Trump's inaugural address on January 20, 2017, was profound in its simplicity: a recognition of the worth of working men and women; a declaration of love of country; a reclamation of self-determination by a people who were taking their country back from the politicians, bureaucrats and financiers. And President Trump's speech was a shot fired across the bow of those whose scheming and self-enrichment had robbed Americans and betrayed the American dream. His speech was a harbinger not merely of a paradigm shift in Washington— but a sea change:

> Today's ceremony, however, has very special meaning because today, we are not merely transferring power from one administration to another or from one party to another, but we are transferring power from Washington, D.C. and giving it back to you, the people.

> For too long, a small group in our nation's capital has reaped the rewards of government while the people have borne the cost. Washington flourished, but the people did not share in its wealth. Politicians prospered, but the jobs left, and the factories closed. The establishment protected itself, but not the citizens of our country. Their victories have not been your victories. Their triumphs have not been your triumphs. And while they celebrated in our nation's capital, there was little to celebrate for struggling families all across our land.

> That all changes starting right here and right now because this moment is your moment, it belongs to you.

> It belongs to everyone gathered here today and everyone watching all across America. This is your day. This is your celebration. And this, the United States of America, is your country.

What truly matters is not which party controls our government, but whether our government is controlled by the people. January 20th, 2017 will be remembered as the day the people became the rulers of this nation again. The forgotten men and women of our country will be forgotten no longer. Everyone is listening to you now.[339]

Ultimately, says Corsi, it was not just Trump that was the enemy to the Deep State— but a sovereign and free America, and its traditional beliefs. Thus, "What Hillary and the hard-left ideology she embraced aimed to destroy was the Judeo-Christian ethics and the free enterprise principles that have been keys to the success of the American experiment."[340] And what was at stake was not just the Presidency, but America: "What is at stake . . . is not just the presidency of Donald J. Trump but the very survival [of] a United States of America that allows the Constitution and our fundamental freedoms to continue for future generations."[341]

In the summer of 2016, months before the Presidential election, the CIA, under Director John Brennan, and the NSA, began surveillance of the Trump campaign. According to Mollie Hemingway of *The Federalist*, the surveillance was not limited to monitoring Carter Page, "It was four top officials [of the Trump Campaign]. They weren't just using FISA wiretaps. They were also using national security letters [which order the release of private information] and human intelligence. At least one human intelligence source."[342]

Thus, in the summer of 2016, the CIA and NSA were spying on the Trump Campaign. The ostensible purpose of the spying was to obtain information that could be used to discredit Trump's campaign— and pave the way for Hillary Clinton to become the 45th President.

There is at least one additional motive for the spying of federal intelligence agencies on the Trump campaign. Under techniques which Robert Mueller helped perfect, federal agencies covertly record conversations without the participants' knowledge. Federal Agents then question the participants in those conversations, about the minute details of secretly recorded conversations. If the participants provide federal agents recollections of the conversations, which differ from the recordings of the conversations, federal authorities may then indict, arrest and convict the participants for lying to federal agents. In this way, federal agencies could obtain the convictions of Trump's Campaign or Executive Staff. Trump's Staff could be convicted for inaccurate statements about previous, covertly recorded conversations— even if they were not guilty of the underlying core offense upon which the investigation was supposedly based. Furthermore, convictions of Staff for the "collateral" offense of inaccurate statements about prior conversations, could be used to pressure Staff members to testify against— or lie about— the President himself.

In short, the first reason for the illicit federal surveillance of the Trump Campaign was to gather information to discredit Donald Trump's campaign, and prevent his election. The second reason was to use covertly recorded conversations to create a spin-off of collateral indictments, arrests and convictions; acquire leverage over indicted witnesses to coerce them into testifying against Donald Trump; and construct a contingency plan to bring charges against Trump in the event he was elected. President Trump's charges that his campaign had been "wiretapped," much ridiculed in the mainstream media, were absolutely true.

Thus, in the summer of 2016, U.S. intelligence agencies conducted illegal federal surveillance and covert recordings of the Trump Campaign. During the same time frame, members of the national intelligence apparatus, led by CIA Director Brennan, manufactured the theme for a media campaign against Donald Trump— the now familiar meme that Trump was guilty of "Russian Collusion," for collaborating with the Russians to rig the election. This media dissimulation was itself a ploy from the psyops bag of tricks of corrupt intelligence operatives. The dark operatives create confusion, and distract attention from themselves, by accusing the opposition of doing the very thing, of which they themselves are guilty.

Corsi details the effort to take Trump out through Special Counsel. Attorney General Jeff Sessions recused himself from the "Russian Collusion" investigations on March 2, 2017. Corsi suggests that Sessions was pressured into recusal, by Congresswoman Nancy Pelosi, and other House Members, because Sessions did not fully disclose his conversations with Russian ambassador Sergey Kislyak in the Senate confirmation hearings on Sessions, and Sessions therefore himself had potential legal exposure. The Recusal of Sessions from the Russian Collusion investigation paved the way for Deputy Attorney General, Rod J. Rosenstein, to take authority over the investigation and name who would serve as Special Counsel for the Russian Collusion investigation. Rosenstein named Robert Mueller as Special Counsel on May 17, 2017. Mueller was not only, as Corsi notes, "widely known in Washington as a . . . Deep State operative."[343] Mueller was long-time, close colleagues with both James

Comey and Rosenstein. Trump had fired Comey on May 9, 2017.[344]

President Trump possesses the constitutional authority to fire Sessions, Rosenstein and Mueller— and thus end the Russian Collusion investigation. However, Congressional liberals, supported by their allies in the mainstream media, threatened to bring impeachment proceedings against Trump in the U.S. House of Representatives, if he fires Sessions, Rosenstein or Mueller.

Thus, Deep State allies in the Congress and media maneuvered to compromise the President, and the Presidency. They pressured Attorney General Sessions to recuse himself from the Russian Collusion investigation, with the charge that he had given incorrect or incomplete testimony to the Senate; thereby paved the way for Deputy Attorney General Rosenstein to decide who would lead the Russian Collusion Investigation as Special Counsel; according to Corsi, lobbied for the appointment of the ethically-challenged Mueller who could be counted on to pursue the Deep State's anti-Trump agenda; and attempted to tie Trump's hands, by threatening to bring impeachment proceedings against him, if he fired any of them— Sessions, Rosenstein or Mueller.[345]

As of August 2018, Mueller's investigation into "Russian Collusion" has produced not one authentic iota of evidence that Donald Trump collaborated with Russia or Russian agents to fix the 2016 Presidential election. Simply stated, there is no credible evidence that Donald Trump is guilty of illegal "Russian Collusion." The irony is that while there is no credible evidence that Donald Trump is guilty of illegal "Russian Collusion," the evidence is overwhelming that the very sponsors and proponents of the Deep State plot to "investigate" Russian Collusion, are themselves guilty of illicit Russian collusion.

Jerome Corsi details the collusion between the Russians, on the one hand, and Mueller and the Clintons, on the other.[346] Kazakhstan, a Central Asian country, is formerly part of the Soviet Union, and is one of the largest uranium producers in the world. Then U.S. Senator Hillary Clinton pressured Kazakhstan officials to sell uranium interests to Canadian investor Frank Giustra. Kazakh officials subsequently sold uranium interests to Giustra in 2005. The following year, Giustra donated $31.3 million to the Clinton Foundation. Giustra followed that with a public pledge to donate an additional $100 million to the Clinton Foundation.

In short, Hillary Clinton pressured Kazakhs to sell lucrative uranium interests to Giustra. Giustra gave scores of millions to the Clinton's Foundation.

Then, in or about 2009, Russia engineered an espionage campaign of bribery and extortion to compromise the Clintons and American officials into allowing Russia to purchase, through an intermediary, uranium interests now owned in America.[347] Russia used a lobbyist to help facilitate the Russian scheme to purchase American-held Uranium interests. The lobbyist, after witnessing Russian suitcases stuffed with $100 bills, became concerned over the illegality of the operation, and reported it to the FBI in or about 2009. Specifically, the lobbyist went to the FBI office in Maryland, the state where the extortion and bribery operation was centered.

The then FBI Director apparently requested that the investigation of the Russian uranium plot be conducted by a

U.S. Attorney in Maryland. FBI Agents and the U.S. Attorney's Office in Maryland investigated and found evidence that Russian emissaries were in fact conducting a campaign of bribery and extortion to gain the leverage necessary to purchase American uranium interests. These federal officials also found evidence that Americans had accepted, and been influenced by, bribes directly or indirectly coming from the Russians.

The then-FBI Director and U.S. Attorney in Maryland could have prevented the sale of American-owned uranium interests to Russia by bringing indictments, by arresting persons participating in the plot, by prosecuting the culpable parties, by notifying the relevant federal oversight agency or even by publicly exposing the scheme. However, the FBI and U.S. Attorney in Maryland did none of those things— no arrests, no indictments, no prosecutions, no convictions, no notifications to the relevant oversight agency, no press releases, no press conferences. Federal officials in Maryland permitted the success of the Russian racketeering scheme to purchase American uranium, and allowed Russia to close the deal. The then-FBI Director and U.S. Attorney in Maryland could have prevented the sale of American-owned uranium interests to Russia. Instead, they effectively did nothing.

The federal officials that were in power when the Russians' closed their illegal purchase of American uranium interests? The FBI Director— Robert Mueller. The then U.S. Attorney in Maryland to whom Mueller himself apparently directed the case— Rod Rosenstein.

Then Secretary of State Hillary Clinton served on the Committee on Foreign Investment in the United States (CFIUS) at the time, a Committee which approves or rejects the foreign purchase of American assets. Uranium One was an American-based company that owned American uranium reserves.

On June 15, 2009, Uranium One purchased half ownership in an asset rich Kazakh uranium holding company. In October of 2010, the CFIUS voted to permit a Russian front company to buy 51% of Uranium One. In effect, the CFIUS approved the Russian purchase of American-owned uranium interests. Mrs. Clinton denies she was involved in the vote. However, Clinton's proxy as the representative of the Office of Secretary of State, cast his vote in favor of the Russian buyout of the Uranium interests. John Podesta was an intimate Clinton ally, and Hillary Clinton's Campaign Manager in the 2016 presidential race. Clinton's proxy who voted for the 2010 Russian buyout of the uranium interests, was arguably rewarded when he was given a Board position with Podesta's Center for American Progress organization.

In 2013, a Russian front company acquired 100% of Uranium One. Again, the CFIUS approved the Russian purchase of American Uranium interests. Corsi notes that "By the time the Russians had acquired 100 percent of Uranium One in 2013, nine of the shareholders in the company had reportedly contributed $145 million in donations to the (Clinton) foundation."[348] According to Corsi's analysis, 100% of Uranium One constitutes 20% of all American uranium holdings; the purchase of 100% of Uranium One is tantamount to the purchase of 20% of all American uranium holdings.

The CFIUS had the authority to nix the Russian purchase of Uranium One. The FBI had been investigating Russian agents since 2009, for attempting to bribe, extort and blackmail their way to ownership of Uranium One. Corsi reports that Mueller and the FBI never notified the CFIUS of the Russians' racketeering operation to acquire Uranium One. Furthermore, notes Corsi, Mueller did nothing as the head of the FBI, to investigate the well over $150 million plus in payments paid to the Clinton Foundation, for apparent involvement in the scheme to sell American uranium interests to the Russians.[349]

In 2010, Bill Clinton was paid a $500,000 speaking fee by Renaissance Capital, for a speech made in Moscow. According to Corsi, Renaissance Capital is a "corporation controlled by former Russian intelligence officers with close ties to Russian President Vladimir Putin."[350]

By the time the dust had settled on the real "Russian Collusion," Russia had purchased 100% of Uranium One; the Clinton Foundation had received $175 to $200 million or more, arguably in payment for the Clintons' help in transferring American uranium interests to Russia; Mueller and Rosenstein ignored evidence of Russian racketeering in the purchase of Uranium One; Mueller and Rosenstein stood down and did nothing to stop the transfer of American uranium interests to Russia despite the obvious underlying criminal conduct of the Russian agents and the patent violation of national interests; Mueller did nothing to investigate the flagrant enrichment of the Clintons as part of the transactions that transferred American uranium interests to the Russia; Bill Clinton got paid $500,000 by Putin's colleagues for a speech in Moscow— and, as Corsi indicates, in obtaining 100% of Uranium One, "Russia gained control of 20 percent of all US uranium production . . . ."[351]

On August 17, 2009, then Secretary of State, Hillary Clinton, transmitted a directive to the U.S. ambassador in Russia, the U.S. ambassador in Tbilisi, Georgia, and the Russian Embassy, stating FBI Director Robert Mueller was going to personally deliver ten grams of highly enriched uranium to Russian law enforcement in Moscow on September 21, 2009. As Corsi reports,

> On June 19, 2017, Shepard Ambellas, the editor in chief of Intellihub.com, noted . . . the classified State Department cable in question that proposed Director Mueller should be the one to personally conduct the transfer of a 10-gram sample of [highly enriched uranium] to Russian law enforcement sources during a secret 'plane-side' meeting on a "tarmac" in early fall of 2009 . . . .[352]

Notes Corsi, "Exactly why Secretary of State Hillary Clinton ordered FBI Director Mueller to make a secret trip to Russia remains shrouded in mystery."[353]

In summary, the Clintons helped the Russians acquire American-held uranium interests; according to Corsi, the Clintons received several hundred million dollars through their Foundation, for the series of transactions through which Russia purchased American-owned uranium; and the Clintons ultimately helped transfer 20% of all U.S. uranium production to the Russians. The FBI, under Mueller's directorate, knew about Russia's illicit effort to acquire American uranium production, and should have known the Clintons were receiving scores of millions of dollars, through their Foundation account, for helping transfer American uranium production to Russia. Yet, the Mueller-led FBI did not indict, arrest, prosecute, convict or expose the Russian perpetrators or their American accomplices, who turned over American uranium production to the Russians; did not inform the CFIUS, the federal agency that oversees the foreign acquisition of American assets, of the Russian racketeering employed to acquire American uranium; did not stop the Russian acquisition of American uranium; did not investigate the Clintons for pocketing $200 million or more, through their Foundation, for the series of transactions that conveyed American uranium to Russia; did not investigate the Clintons for their role in transferring 20% of American uranium production to a foreign country. And Mueller, at the directive of Hillary Clinton, as Secretary of State, personally transmitted highly enriched uranium to Moscow, to hand to the Russians.

As for Donald Trump? Mueller has led the "Russian Collusion" investigation into Donald Trump for over 15 months, and has had at his disposal significant staff and resources, and the full panoply of Orwellian Mass Surveillance techniques which Mueller himself helped devise. Yet, Mueller has produced not one shred of credible evidence that Donald Trump was guilty of illegal "Russian Collusion" in rigging the 2016 election.

The Clintons and Mueller are palpably guilty of illicit Russian collusion. Donald Trump is ostensibly innocent of illicit Russian collusion. In an inversion of logic and morality, and the use of a standard psyop ploy, the perpetrators are accusing the innocent of a crime which the perpetrators themselves committed. Mr. Mueller was appointed to investigate Donald Trump for "Russian Collusion." It is Mueller himself, who is guilty of Russian Collusion.

FBI counterintelligence Agent Peter Strzok played a key role in shielding Hillary Clinton from prosecution for her use of a private server for State Department business. Strzok was present at the FBI's July 2, 2016 Interview of Hillary Clinton. Important steps were taken at that interview to insulate Clinton from prosecution. Clinton was not placed under oath. No verbatim transcript was made of the Interview. Further steps were taken by Strzok to ensure Clinton was not charged. Strzok apparently participated in the decisions to grant immunity to top Clinton staff, to preclude them from being indicted and pressured to testify about what they knew about Hillary Clinton. As Corsi reports, "Strzok appears to have been involved in a series of FBI decisions that granted immunity to key Clinton aides involved with the private email server controversy . . . ."[354] Strzok famously changed the wording of a public statement made by James Comey on July 5, 2016, from declaring that Hillary Clinton was "grossly negligent" in handling classified information— a federal crime— to stating simply that Clinton was "extremely careless" with the information— not a federal crime.

As Corsi reports, Strzok and FBI attorney Lisa Page exchanged some 10,000 text messages from August 2015 to December 2016.[355] These texts revealed the loathing of Donald Trump by Strzok and Page. They further suggested the broad outlines of the Deep State effort to prevent Hillary Clinton from being criminally prosecuted for the illegal handling of classified information. These texts also betrayed an intent to implement a contingency plan, in case Trump was elected, to derail his presidency with the fabricated accusation that Trump had colluded with the Russians to rig the election. As Corsi asserts, the text messages "strongly suggested the FBI and DOJ had conspired to prevent Hillary Clinton from being prosecuted over her email scandal while simultaneously setting up the pretext that Donald Trump had colluded with Russia to prevent Trump for serving as president should he win the 2016 election."[356]

As Corsi cogently summarizes,

What Strzok's message makes clear is that Page and Strzok, in the presence of a high-ranking FBI official, had laid out an "insurance policy" plan to make sure Trump never served his term as president, even if Trump pulled off a miracle to win the election and beat Strzok and Page's clear favorite Hillary Clinton. Soon it developed that the "insurance policy" involved the Russian collusion evidence the FBI had been quietly accumulating against the Trump campaign. The frightening prospect conveyed by Strzok's text message was that a small group of politically biased FBI officials at the very top of the organization were determined to both make sure Hillary was never indicted or prosecuted, and make sure sufficient evidence to impeach Trump was available in the unlikely event he should be elected president.[357]

Deep State had a plan in place, before the 2016 election, to accuse Donald Trump of Russian Collusion, in the event Trump was elected. In August 2017, after Mueller learned of the text messaging between Strzok and Page, Strzok was removed from Mueller's Special Counsel Staff, and reassigned to the FBI's Human Relations Department. In late September of 2017, Mueller removed Lisa Page from his team.

Mueller did not reveal to the President, Congress or the American people why Strzok and Page were fired from his team. Mueller did not disclose their personal bias and plotting against the President. Mueller did not release the text messages between Strzok and Page. Mueller did not reveal the crucial role Strzok played in insulating Trump's electoral foe, Hillary Clinton, from prosecution. Mueller did not reveal

149

the "insurance policy"— the plan formulated before the election to accuse Donald Trump of Russian Collusion if he were elected.

As Corsi notes, the true reason behind the dismissal of Strzok and Page remained a mystery, "until December 2017, when the DOJ shared with Congress a sample of 375 text messages from the 10,000 messages Inspector General Horowitz found Strzok and Page had exchanged between August 2015 and December 2016."[358] In short, the lead investigator, Mueller, covered up the inherent bias of the investigation. Thus, notes Corsi, "Both Special Counsel Mueller and Deputy Attorney General Rod Rosenstein . . . had covered up all information about the Strzok-Page text messages in order to hide from the public the amount of anti-Trump hatred . . . at the head of the FBI and DOJ during the election and afterward . . . ."[359]

Deep State operatives have not uncovered evidence that Donald Trump was guilty of illegal collusion with the Russians relative to the 2016 Presidential election. On March 5, 2017, Director of National Intelligence James Clapper told *NBC News* that a federal interagency report documented no evidence of collusion between the Trump campaign and Russian officials. As Clapper told NBC, "we did not include any evidence in our report, and I say 'our' that's NSA, FBI and CIA, with my office, the Director of National Intelligence, that had anything, that had any reflection of collusion between members of the Trump campaign and the Russians. There was no evidence of that included in our report."[360] As Corsi further records, "On May 8, 2017, . . . Clapper told a Senate judiciary subcommittee under oath that he had not seen any evidence of collusion between the Trump campaign and Russian officials."[361]

150

The fact that there is no evidence of Russian Collusion by Trump or his Campaign, even the fact that Trump is demonstrably innocent of the allegation, is apparently irrelevant to Mueller, and his investigation, which keeps rolling along. In fact, the absence of evidence, appears to have driven Mueller and his subordinates to strive even harder to build a case. As Mark Penn, a former advisor to President Clinton has commented, in *The Hill*, on May 20, 2018:

> The president's earlier legal team was naive in believing that, when Mueller found nothing, he would just end it. Instead, the less investigators found, the more determined and expansive they became.
>
> * * * *
>
> . . . . Rather than a fair, limited and impartial investigation, the Mueller investigation became a partisan, open-ended inquisition that, by its precedent, is a threat to all those who ever want to participate in a national campaign or an administration again.[362]

Indeed, Mueller's attack on President Trump was always a multi-faceted strategy to take out the President, by whatever means, at whatever the cost, with whatever the moral implications or national consequences. Mueller's immediate mission was to present the accusation, regardless of merit, that Trump collaborated with the Russians to win the election. The accusation of Russian collusion was the tactical and thematic predicate for both a ***political/media*** attack on Trump, and a ***legal*** assault. Actual guilt or innocence had nothing to do with it. Mueller is palpably impervious to the fact that true evidence is uncovered— not "developed."

Under the *political/media* attack, as described by Corsi, Mueller would level the charge of Russian Collusion, make strategic leaks to the mass media, and attempt to drive Trump into resignation by media-manipulated public opinion.[363]   Under a second political/media stratagem, Mueller would beat the media drum with the Russia Collusion meme, long enough and hard enough, to impel Congress to impeach President Trump.[364] Under a third political/media stratagem, Mueller would repeat the Russian Collusion accusation with enough frequency, and with sufficient media echo, to press the political case that President Trump is unstable, mentally incompetent, and subject to removal from Office under the 25th Amendment.[365]

Mueller's *legal* strategy, like Mueller's *political/media* strategy, encompasses at least three prongs of attack. And like Mueller's political/media strategy, Mueller's legal strategy is not deterred by the fact that there is no evidence that Trump colluded with the Russians to rig the 2016 Presidential Election.

In fact, Mueller's legal strategy is intentionally designed to bring down the President, even if the President is not guilty. As McGovern and Binney write, "After a year of investigating whether the Trump campaign colluded with Russia, Special Counsel Robert Mueller has, in effect, admitted that he has hit a dry well."[366]   As Calvin Fields has noted, "Mueller is trying to pin any crime he can manufacture on our president . . . ."[367]   Because there is no credible evidence that President Trump colluded with Russia to fix the election, Mueller has had to both fall back on his corrupt, yet proven practices, and also be creative, in order to indict the President for a crime he did not commit.

Mueller's three primary legal strategies:

1. Indict the President for Obstruction of Justice for firing James Comey— even though the President has clear constitutional authority to do just that, and even though Deputy Attorney General Rod Rosenstein has admitted Trump had grounds to fire Comey.

2. The long-abused practice of indicting other persons, and pressuring them to testify against, even lie against, the primary target, in order to avoid incarceration. The diabolism of this approach is exacerbated by Mueller's favored practice of covertly recording communications with pervasive surveillance; questioning witnesses about past conversations they may vaguely remember or wish to deny; and then charging the witnesses with federal crimes if they make inaccurate statements to federal agents about the fact or content of past, recorded conversations.

3. Because Mueller cannot come up with a credible case that the President colluded with the Russians to rig the election, Mueller could also attempt to maneuver the President into the perjury trap, described above in Strategy Number 2. Under this approach, Mueller is trying to bait the President to submit to an Interview with federal agents; get the President to make a statement which Mueller could tell a Grand Jury was false; and therefore, manufacture an indictment of the President of the United States for making a false statement to federal investigators.

Ray McGovern and Bill Binney, long time federal intelligence agents both, have described the treacherous chess game, Mueller has designed to depose the President.[368] From Mueller's perspective, indicting the President on collateral charges of making false statements to federal agents is necessary to Mueller's self-preservation, because the charge that Trump colluded with the Russians is false, and Mueller is anxious to obtain Trump's scalp on other grounds— any grounds— so he doesn't have to publicly admit the investigation was a scam from the outset. In short, because Mueller doesn't have a case against Trump for Russian Collusion, he wants Trump to give an interview to federal agents, so Mueller can indict Trump for making false statements to the Feds.

As McGovern and Binney observe, "[I]t does not appear likely that [Mueller] is going to get his man this time. So, rather than throw in the towel, [Mueller] is making a college try at cajoling President Donald Trump into helping him out."[369]   Mueller's effort "bespeaks an embarrassingly desperate attempt to get President Donald Trump to incriminate himself."[370]   McGovern and Binney derisively describe a *New York Times* editorial seeking to dignify Mueller's desperate attempt to salvage an inherently fraudulent investigation:

> (T)he *Times* explains that "Mr. Preibus, who was Trump's chief of staff, has said he raced out of the White House after Mr. Sessions and implored him not to resign. Mr. Mueller has interviewed Mr. Priebus and would be able to compare his answer with those of Mr. Trump." Aha!   Might this be a clue to Mueller's approach?   Something informally called The Flynn-Papadopolous Playbook for Dummies? What if the President's recollection does not exactly match that of Preibus?   A gotcha moment? Perjury.[371]

As McGovern and Binney further point out, Mueller's efforts to get Trump to speak to federal investigators so Mueller can manufacture an indictment for making false statements to federal Agents, is the most graphic admission of all: Mueller has no "Russian Collusion" case against Trump. As McGovern and Binney have written:

> Mueller knows better than anyone, where and how to find the dirt on the Trump campaign, collusion with Russia, or anything else. That he has been able to come up with so little— and is trying to get some help from the President himself— speaks volumes.

> Mueller does not need to send his team off on a "broad quest" with "open-ended" inquiries on an "exhaustive array of subjects." If there were any tangible evidence of Trump campaign-Russia collusion, Mueller would almost certainly have known where to look and, in today's world of blanket surveillance, would have found it by now. It beggars belief that he would have failed, in the course of his year-old investigation, to use all the levers at his disposal— the levers Edward Snowden called "turnkey tyranny"— to "get the goods" on Trump.[372]

Concluded McGovern and Binney: "Never before has it been clearer that the Mueller investigation is 90 percent charade."[373]

Corsi dissects Mueller's three pronged *political/media* strategy to destroy the Trump Presidency: a Media Campaign, based upon the false meme of Russian Collusion, to mobilize public opinion to drive the President to resignation; a Media Campaign to impel Congress to impeach; a fatuous effort, powered by the mass media echo chambers, to make the case that President Trump is mentally unstable, and thus "unable to discharge the powers and duties of his office"[374] under the 25th Amendment.[375] William Binney, Ray McGovern and others have described the trident of Mueller's' *legal* strategy to shipwreck the 45th Presidency: the filing of Obstruction of Justice charges for firing Comey, even though it was an Action which the President was constitutionally entitled to take; the indictment of subordinates, even on unrelated charges, to pressure them into testifying against the President; setting the President up for the "perjury trap" by coercing him to submit to an interview by federal investigators, so that Mueller can indict the President for making false statements to investigators, irrespective of the accuracy of the President's statements.[376]

Phil Mudd is the former FBI Deputy Director to Robert Mueller. In a televised interview with CNN on August 10, 2017, Mudd complained about Trump's treatment of CIA Agents and State Department employees. Stated Mudd, "Let me give you bottom line as a former government official. *Government is going to kill this guy*."[377] Stated Mudd later in the same interview, "*The government is going to kill this guy* because he doesn't support them."[378]

As Corsi makes clear, the Deep State and its minion Mueller are willing to employ *political/media* stratagems to take out the President, no matter how duplicitous the strategy; and the Deep State and Mueller are willing to use *legal* strategies to wreck this Presidency, no matter how fraudulent their method. But according to Corsi, Deep State is willing to implement one other course to destroy the 45th President:

Should the Deep State fail to remove Trump from office through impeachment or a charge under the 25th Amendment that he is mentally incompetent "executive action"—a CIA plan to assassinate Trump is the Deep State's last resort.[379]

* * * *

The Deep State will not care if Trump is impeached, declared mentally incompetent, or— as a final resort— assassinated, as long as he is removed from office before the completion of his first term.[380]

Chapter 11

A Tale of Two Muellers

Robert Mueller, according to many in the mainstream media, and among the politically correct, is an on-time, button down, pressed white shirt, by-the-book, Eagle Scout, Straight Arrow. The description of Mueller by Darrell Samuelsohn of *Politico* on October 2, 2017, could be set to music:

> Robert Mueller is rarely seen and almost never heard. He doesn't frequent popular restaurants, appear on television or even issue statements. When he meets in person with President Donald Trump's lawyers, he does not visit the White House where reporters might notice. He instead summons them to the conference rooms of his southwest Washington, D.C., office, the specific location of which is among his many well-guarded secrets.[381]

According to Samuelsohn, Mueller told a Washington lawyer, "I play it by the book and I tell anyone who works with me you better play it by the book."[382]

It is difficult to square Samuelsohn's velvet gloves treatment with Mueller's 30-year track record of treachery and deceit. More authentic than Samuelsohn's statement, is the question posed by Jon Bowne in an *InfoWars* broadcast on July 8, 2018:

Who is Special Counsel Robert Mueller?

Is he the upstanding career law enforcement officer as the establishment would lead you to believe?

Or is Robert Mueller a dirty fixit man for the corrupt authoritarians lurking behind the D.C. Power Structure?[383]

Jesus counseled over 2,000 years ago:

> ***Beware of false prophets, who come to you in sheep's clothing, but inwardly they are ravening wolves.***
>
> ***Ye shall know them by their fruits.***
> (Matthew 7:15-16)

It is difficult to reconcile the Robert Mueller who has left a decades-long trail of broken lives and betrayals, with the pristine, alabaster image depicted by the mass media and powerful politicians.

Chapter 12

Mueller's World: A Moral Inversion

Mueller's work of the last 30 years speaks for itself. And that work includes cover-ups he led, and those in which he lent a hand; crimes he concealed and criminals for which he covered up; investigations he obstructed and victims he abused.

In one way or another, Mueller has left his unmistakable imprint on: The federal protection of Mafia Kingpin Whitey Bulger and his gang in Boston and keeping one or more innocent men in prison to rot. The federal coverup of the Pan Am 103 bombing. The shielding of BCCI Principals from criminal prosecution for bankrolling and laundering money for drug traffickers, illegal arms merchants and corrupt intelligence agents. The implicit apologetics for the actions of federal agents in slaying Vicki Weaver and her 14-year-old son, and shooting her unarmed husband in the back. The obstruction of the investigation into 9-11, the active coverup of Saudi involvement in the crime, the lie to the nation that the government had no forewarning of the 9-11 attacks. The apparent falsification of charges in the Anthrax case, which conveniently allowed the true perpetrators to go undetected. The false testimony to Congress that Iraq had weapons of mass destruction, to help build the case for War in Iraq. The untrue testimony to Congress that mass surveillance was necessary to prevent 9-11, when in fact 9-11 could have been stopped in its tracks if intelligence bureaucrats had listened to the federal agents on the street. The attempt to sabotage the Trump Presidency with a false allegation of Russian collusion, when in fact it was Mueller and the Clintons that had colluded with Russia to transfer 20% of America's uranium to Russia.

Mueller's career stands unapologetically for the proposition that, when it comes to protecting covert operations or advancing secret agendas, human beings are collateral damage. He has shown a willingness to trample the Bible, shred the Constitution and incinerate organic charters of human rights. And he has evinced a pathological disregard for the ordinary citizens that the Holy Writ and these unequalable documents were meant to protect. Citizens that get in the way of covert ops or illicit government schemes are simply collateral damage.

And the list of those that constitute collateral damage is too lengthy, to abide or absorb. The children of Louie Greco whose lives were destroyed when their father died in prison for a murder committed by the federally protected Bulger gang. Charles McKee, on his way home to blow the whistle on a CIA drug ring, who died among 269 others, in a plane wreck, which Mueller helped coverup. It was this same Charles McKee whose suitcase was rifled, as his fellow federal agents, presumably under Mueller's control, stepped over the wreckage and dead bodies to destroy the evidence of a CIA black op drug ring operating out of the Middle East. Vicki Weaver shot to death by a federal sniper in Ruby Ridge, while standing in the door of her home, unarmed, holding her 10-month-old daughter— with Mueller incensed by the criticism of her killing. The hapless immigrants in New York, detained and abused for months, under Mueller's direct supervision, for 9-11 attacks with which they were uninvolved, after Mueller helped whisk the cadre of bin Ladens and high-ranking Saudis, most likely connected to the crime, out of the country. The families of 9-11 victims whom Mueller betrayed, by obstructing the investigation of the criminal conspiracy that killed their loved ones. Dr. Bruce Ivins, who committed suicide, or was killed, and the timing of whose death was convenient for the Mueller-led investigation, that couldn't get the evidence to fit the accusation that Ivins was the anthrax killer. The millions of Americans who have had their right to private— and free— communications, movements and actions stolen by Mueller's twisted vision of a relentless Surveillance State. David Graham, who was poisoned, after he would not keep silent about the fact that two of the Saudi terrorists were living in Shreveport, Louisiana before 9-11, Graham reported them to the feds— and Federal authorities did nothing.

Over time, the hallmarks of a Mueller operation clearly emerge: Persecute the innocent. Let culprits and killers go free. Cover for covert operations, no matter how immoral. Punish whistleblowers. Reward wrongdoing. Use the weapons at hand to worship the State: misleading leaks, intimidation of witnesses, destruction of documents, bribery— and lies. In Mueller's World, the Truth itself is collateral damage.

In this upside-down, covert kingdom, human freedom, human dignity, human lives, may be sacrificed on the altar of black ops, international politics, the privileges and preferences of the power elite. Mueller has no regard for this seminal Truth: The Rule of Law does not signify unquestioned obeisance to persons of power, but undying respect to precepts of Principle. Capitulation to persons simply because they embody the power of Law, when they themselves abrogate the law, is not respect for the Rule of Law at all— but its bipartite antithesis, dictatorship and slavery. When the Rule of Law is properly understood, Mueller's body of work demonstrates that this celebrated federal law enforcement officer is not only against freedom, and against the sanctity of human life. He is against the Rule of Law itself.

That Mueller has come to be seen as some unsung champion of American values, chosen to represent the national interests in a Collision of Constitutional values, and a monumentally historic showdown, is a commentary on the lassitude of the mainstream media— indeed, of all of us.

However, the relevant narrative is not merely that Mueller wields the power of the State against the people. The transcendent saga, ultimately, is the courage of federal agents, career intelligence officers, writers, soldiers, police officers, veterans, elected officials, family members of victims, Congressmen and Senators, ordinary citizens, who have defied and resisted the Deep State's attack on truth. Many are the Federal agents and journalists, often painted with a broad brush of disrepute, who have risked all, and sacrificed much, to tell the truth, and demand Justice.

The Psalmist lamented the powerful wicked:

For I was envious at the foolish, when I saw the prosperity of the wicked.
For there are no bands in their death: but their strength is firm.
They are not in trouble as other men; neither are they plagued like other men.
Therefore pride compasseth them about as a chain; violence covereth them as a garment.
Their eyes stand out with fatness: they have more than heart could wish.
They are corrupt, and speak wickedly concerning oppression: they speak loftily.

They set their mouth against the heavens, and
their tongue walketh through the earth.
(Psalms 73:3-8)

But there is hope for Justice.

Until I went into the sanctuary of God; then
understood I their end.
Surely thou didst set them in slippery places:
thou castedst them down into destruction.
How are they brought into desolation, as in a
moment! they are utterly consumed with terrors.
(Psalms 73:17-19)

When America passed through the epic Crucibles of
the last 30 years, Mr. Mueller could be continually counted
upon, to tell untruths, do the wrong thing, avert his eyes from
evil. Yet it was Robert Mueller, whom Deputy Attorney
General Rosenstein appointed, to carry the morally,
constitutionally and civically monumental burden of
investigating the President of the United States.

There is an existential conundrum between this
burden, and Mr. Mueller's biography. His actions are not
characterized merely by moral atrophy— but by moral
inversion. Indeed, Robert Mueller has become a type of
Morally Inverse, Man for All Seasons. His is a trajectory of
acclaim. That trajectory has been a pathway of pain for
others.

Robert Mueller has relentlessly abused his power and
position to advance the agenda of the power elite, as a Deep
State minion, a clandestine schemer— an amoral Errand Boy
for the New World Order.

Chapter 1 *Tributes, Trajectory and Treason*

1.   *USA TODAY,* William G. Otis (June 14, 2017).
2.   "Mueller's History of Cover-Ups," *Dig Within,* Kevin Ryan (April 8, 2018).
3.   "Robert Mueller Is an Amoral Legal Assassin: He Will Do His Job If You Let Him," *LaRouchePAC,* Barbara Boyd (September 27, 2017).
4.   *Id.*
5.   *Id.*
6.   "10 Things to Hate About Mueller," *Foreign Policy,* Benjamin Wittes, Susan Hennessey (September 20, 2017)
7.   *Id.*
8.   *Id.*
9.   "Sean Hannity compares Robert Mueller to Stalin's Secret Police Chief in Latest Attack on Trump-Russia Investigation," *Newsweek.com,* Jason Le Miere (August 21, 2018)
10.   *Id.*
11.   "It's Official . . . Robert Mueller is a Bad Guy," *Patriotheadquarters.com*

Chapter 2 *Whitey Bulger Gang*

12.   "Probing Mueller: What Were His Roles in Boston Mafia Murders, Uranium One, and Other FBI Scandals?" *The New American*, William F. Jasper (March 22, 2018).
13.   "FBI Covering for Criminals," *The New American,* William F. Jasper (June 22, 1998).
14.   "A Lingering Question for the FBI's Director," *The Boston Globe*, Kevin Cullen (July 14, 2011).
15.   *Id.*
16.   "Probing Mueller: What Were His Roles in Boston Mafia Murders, Uranium One, and Other FBI Scandals?" *The New American*, William F. Jasper (March 22, 2018).

17.   *Id.*
18.   "Questions Still Surround Robert Mueller's Boston Past," Sara A. Carter, (March 19, 2018).
19.   "FBI Covering for Criminals," *The New American,* William F. Jasper (June 22, 1998).
20.   *Id.*
21.   *Id.*
22.   *Id.*
23.   "Probing Mueller: What Were His Roles in Boston Mafia Murders, Uranium One, and Other FBI Scandals?" *The New American*, William F. Jasper (March 22, 2018) (emphasis in Original)
24.   "FBI Covering for Criminals," *The New American,* William F. Jasper (June 22, 1998).
25.   "A Lingering Question for the FBI's Director," *The Boston Globe*, Kevin Cullen (July 14, 2011).
26.   "FBI Covering for Criminals," *The New American,* William F. Jasper (June 22, 1998).
27.   *Id.*
28.   *Id.*
29.   *Id.*
30.   *Id.*
31.   "The Murder Case That Never Ends, The Crime That Keeps On Giving," *WBUR News*, David Boeri (June 30, 2010).
32.   "Probing Mueller: What Were His Roles in Boston Mafia Murders, Uranium One, and Other FBI Scandals?" *The New American*, William F. Jasper (March 22, 2018).
33.   "Questions Still Surround Robert Mueller's Boston Past," Sara A. Carter, (March 19, 2018).
34.   "Probing Mueller: What Were His Roles in Boston Mafia Murders, Uranium One, and Other FBI Scandals?" *The New American*, William F. Jasper (March 22, 2018).
35.   "A Lingering Question for the FBI's Director," *The Boston Globe*, Kevin Cullen (July 14, 2011).
36.   *Id.*

37.   "The Murder Case That Never Ends, The Crime That Keeps On Giving," *WBUR News*, David Boeri (June 30, 2010).
38.   *Id.*
39.   *Id.*
40.   *Id.*
41.   *Id.*
42.   *Id.*
43.   *Id.*
44.   *Id.*
45.   *Id.*
46.   *Id.*
47.   *Id.*
48.   "Probing Mueller: What Were His Roles in Boston Mafia Murders, Uranium One, and Other FBI Scandals?" *The New American*, William F. Jasper (March 22, 2018).
49.   "A Lingering Question for the FBI's Director," *The Boston Globe*, Kevin Cullen (July 14, 2011).
50.   *Id.*
51.   *Id.*
52.   "Probing Mueller: What Were His Roles in Boston Mafia Murders, Uranium One, and Other FBI Scandals?" *The New American*, William F. Jasper (March 22, 2018).
53.   "A Lingering Question for the FBI's Director," *The Boston Globe*, Kevin Cullen (July 14, 2011).

Chapter 3 *Pan Am 103*

54.   "Pan Am Flight 103/ Lockerbie Air Disaster Archives," *Pan Am Flight 103/Lockerbie Air Disaster Archives*, (2010).
55.   "Pan Am 103 Why Did They Die?" *TIME Magazine*, Roy Rowan (June 24, 2001).
56.   "Pan Am Flight 103/ Lockerbie Air Disaster Archives," *Pan Am Flight 103/Lockerbie Air Disaster Archives*, (2010).

57. *Id.*
58. "FLIGHT 103: The OTHER Story," Erick Anderson (June 8, 1999).
59. "Pan Am Flight 103" *Left Hook,* Dean Henderson.
60. "Lockerbie Doubts," *Consortiumnews.com*, Lisa Pease (May 23, 2012).
61. "Pan Am 103 Why Did They Die?" *TIME Magazine*, Roy Rowan (June 24, 2001).
62. "Lockerbie Doubts," *Consortiumnews.com*, Lisa Pease (May 23, 2012).
63. "Pan Am 103 Why Did They Die?" *TIME Magazine*, Roy Rowan (June 24, 2001).
64. *Id.*
65. *Id.*
66. *Id.*
67. *Id.*
68. "Lockerbie Doubts," *Consortiumnews.com*, Lisa Pease (May 23, 2012).
69. "Pan Am 103 Why Did They Die?" *TIME Magazine*, Roy Rowan (June 24, 2001).
70. "FLIGHT 103: The OTHER Story," Erick Anderson (June 8, 1999).
71. *Id.*
72. "Bombing of Pan Am Flight 103 Over Lockerbie: the Truth!" *LinkedIn*, Rodney Stich (August 30, 2014).
73. "Tehran Hands Over the Remaining Funds to Jibril PFLP-GC," *OhmyNews International*, Ludwig DeBraeckeleer (December 31, 2008).
74. *Id.*
75. *Id.*
76. *Id.*
77. *Id.*
78. *Id.*
79. *Id.*
80. *Id.*
81. *Id.*
82. *Id.*

83.   "Pan Am 103 Why Did They Die?" *TIME Magazine*, Roy Rowan (June 24, 2001).

84.   *Id.*

85.   *Id.*

86.   *Id.*

87.   "FLIGHT 103: The OTHER Story," Erick Anderson (June 8, 1999).

88.   *Lockerbietruth.com*, Jim Swire and Peter Biddolph; "Huge Miles: Lockerbie: What was it Iran? Syria? All I know is, it wasn't the man in prison," *INDEPENDENT*, Hugh Miles (December 21, 2008).

89.   "The Framing of Al-Megrahi: The Death of Justice." *London Review of Books*, Gareth Peirce (May 20, 2012).

90.   "FLIGHT 103: The OTHER Story," Erick Anderson (June 8, 1999).

91.   *Id.* (emphasis added)

92.   *Id.*

93.   *Id.*

94.   "Pan Am 103 Why Did They Die?" *TIME Magazine*, Roy Rowan (June 24, 2001).

95.   *Id.*

96.   "FLIGHT 103: The OTHER Story," Erick Anderson (June 8, 1999).

97.   *Id.*

98.   *Id.*

99.   "Pan Am Flight 103," *Left Hook,* Dean Henderson.

100.   "Lockerbie Doubts," *Consortiumnews.com*, Lisa Pease (May 23, 2012).

101.   "Pan Am 103 Why Did They Die?" *TIME Magazine*, Roy Rowan (June 24, 2001).

102.   *Id.*

103.   *Id.*

104.   "Pan Am Flight 103," *Left Hook,* Dean Henderson.

105.   "The Framing of Al-Megrahi: The Death of Justice," *London Review of Books*, Gareth Peirce (May 20, 2012).

106. "Lockerbie Doubts," *Consortiumnews.com*, Lisa Pease (May 23, 2012).

107. "Flight 103: A Solution Assembled From Fragments and Debris," *The New York Times*, David Johnston (November 15, 1991).

108. "Lockerbie: the Flight from Justice," *Pressdram*, Paul Foot (2001).

109. "Pan Am 103 Why Did They Die?" *TIME Magazine*, Roy Rowan (June 24, 2001).

110. "Lockerbie: the Flight from Justice," *Pressdram*, Paul Foot (2001).

111. "Charles McKee's Suitcase," *The Lockerbie Divide* (September 17, 2010)

112. *Id.*

113. *Id.*

114. *Id.*

115. "FLIGHT 103: The OTHER Story," Erick Anderson (June 8, 1999).

116. "Lockerbie Doubts," *Consortiumnews.com*, Lisa Pease (May 23, 2012).

117. "Pan Am 103 Why Did They Die?" *TIME Magazine*, Roy Rowan (June 24, 2001).

118. "Lockerbie Bombing: CIA Believes 'to a Man' That Iran Carried out Attack on Pan Am Flight 103, Says Former Agent," *The Telegraph,* Gordon Rayner (March 11, 2014).

119. *Id.*

120. *Id.*

121. *Id.*

122. *Lockerbietruth.com*, Jim Swire and Peter Biddolph.

123. "Pan Am 103 Why Did They Die?" *TIME Magazine*, Roy Rowan (June 24, 2001).

124. "Pan Am Flight 103," *Left Hook,* Dean Henderson.

125. "Pan Am 103 Why Did They Die?" *TIME Magazine*, Roy Rowan (June 24, 2001).

126. "Mueller's History of Cover-Ups," *Dig Within*, Kevin Ryan (April 8, 2018).

127. "A Tale of Three Atrocities," *The Lockerbie Divide*, Charles Norrie (August 20, 2010).
128. "Pan Am 103 Why Did They Die?" *TIME Magazine*, Roy Rowan (June 24, 2001).
129. *Id.*
130. *Id.*
131. *Id.*
132. "Lockerbie Doubts," *Consortiumnews.com*, Lisa Pease (May 23, 2012).
133. *Id.*
134. *Id.*
135. *Id.*
136. "Pan Am 103 Why Did They Die?" *TIME Magazine*, Roy Rowan (June 24, 2001).
137. "Lockerbie Doubts," *Consortiumnews.com*, Lisa Pease (May 23, 2012).
138. *Id.*
139. *Id.*
140. *Id.*
141. *Id.*
142. *Id.*
143. "Lockerbie Doubts," *Consortiumnews.com*, Lisa Pease (May 23, 2012).
144. "Pan Am Flight 103," *Left Hook,* Dean Henderson.
145. "Pan Am 103 Why Did They Die?" *Time*, Roy Rowan (June 24, 2001).
146. "Pan Am Flight 103," *Left Hook,* Dean Henderson.
147. "Mueller's History of Cover-Ups," *Dig Within,* Kevin Ryan (April 8, 2018).
148. *Id.*
149. "Pan Am 103 Why Did They Die?" *TIME Magazine*, Roy Rowan (June 24, 2001).
150. *Id.*
151. *Id.*
152. *Id.*
153. *Id.*
154. *Id.*

155. *Id.*
156. *Id.*
157. *Id.*
158. *Id.*
159. *Id.*
160. "The Framing of Al-Megrahi: The Death of Justice," *London Review of Books*, Gareth Peirce (May 20, 2012).
161. *Id.*
162. *Id.*
163. "Lockerbie Doubts," *Consortiumnews.com*, Lisa Pease (May 23, 2012).
164. "The Framing of Al-Megrahi: The Death of Justice," *London Review of Books*, Gareth Peirce (May 20, 2012).
165. "Report on Identification Procedures: Abdelbasset Ali Mohmed al-Megrahi v. H.M. Advocate," Report of Steven E. Clark, Professor of Psychology at the University of California.
166. "The Framing of Al-Megrahi: The Death of Justice," *London Review of Books*, Gareth Peirce (May 20, 2012).
167. *Id.*
168. *Id.*
169. *Id.*
170. *Id.*
171. "Lockerbie Revisited," Documentary Directed by Gideon Levy (April 27, 2009)
172. *Id.*
173. "The Framing of Al-Megrahi: The Death of Justice," *London Review of Books*, Gareth Peirce (May 20, 2012).
174. "Lockerbie Revisited," Videodocumentary by Gideon Levy, (broadcast April 27, 2009).
175. "Lockerbie Doubts," *Consortiumnews.com*, Lisa Pease (May 23, 2012).

176. "The Framing of Al-Megrahi: The Death of Justice," *London Review of Books*, Gareth Peirce (May 20, 2012).
177. *Id.*
178. *Id.*
179. *Id.*
180. *Id.*
181. "Mueller's History of Cover-Ups," *Dig Within*, Kevin Ryan (April 8, 2018).

Chapter 4 *BCCI*

182. "Essay; B.C.C.I.: Justice Delayed." *The New York Times,* William Safire (July 25, 1991).
183. "Questions for Mr. Mueller." *The Wall Street Journal,* Muriel Kane (June 26, 2001).
184. "Mueller's History of Cover-Ups," *Dig Within,* Kevin Ryan (April 8, 2018).
185. Questions for Mr. Mueller." *The Wall Street Journal,* Muriel Kane (June 26, 2001).
186. "Bush, Bin Laden, BCCI and the 9/11 Commission." *Counter Punch*, Chris Floyd (October 12, 2015).
187. "Questions for Mr. Mueller." *The Wall Street Journal,* Muriel Kane (June 26, 2001).
188. *Id.*
189. "Bush, Bin Laden, BCCI and the 9/11 Commission." *Counter Punch*, Chris Floyd (October 12, 2015).
190. "Robert Mueller Is an Amoral Legal Assassin: He Will Do His Job If You Let Him." *LaRouchePAC*, Barbara Boyd (September 27, 2017).

Chapter 5 *Ruby Ridge*

191. "Man in the News; A Man Made for Law Enforcement — Robert Swan Mueller III." *The New York Times*, Neil Lewis (July 6, 2001).

192. "Mueller's History of Cover-Ups," *Dig Within,* Kevin Ryan (April 8, 2018).
193. "Bin Laden Family Evacuated." *CBS News*, CBS News Staff (September 30, 2001).
194. *Id.*
195. "After 9/11: the Saudis Who Slipped Away." *Los Angeles Times*, Craig Unger (April 11, 2004).
196. *Id.*
197. *Id.*
198. *Id.*
199. Speech of Robert Mueller to Commonwealth Club of California, (April 19, 2002).
200. *Id.*
201. *Id.*
202. *Id.*
203. "TRACES OF TERRORISM: THE WARNINGS; F.B.I. Knew for Years About Terror Pilot Training," *The New York Times*, Phillip Shenon (May 18, 2002).
204. "CIA Warned Of U.S. Attack In '95." *CBS News*, Rebecca Leung (March 21, 2004).
205. "Another Dot That Didn't Get Connected/Newsweek Report: CIA Dropped Ball on Hijackers." *SFGate,* Zachary Coile (June 3, 2002).
206. "What Happened? Bush Was Warned of Hijackings Before 9/11," *ABC News,* ABC News Staff (May 16, 2002).
207. "Bush Knew of the Terrorist Plot to Hijack US Planes," *The Guardian*, Jason Burke and Ed Vulliamy (May 18, 2002).
208. "Condoleezza Rice Warned Sept. 6 about Imminent Terror Attack," *NewsMax.com*, Carl Limbacher (May 29, 2002).
209. "The Deafness Before the Storm." *The New York Times,* Kurt Eichenwald (September 11, 2012).
210. *Id.*
211. "Two New FBI Missteps Reported," *CBS News*, Jaime Holguin (June 2, 2002).

212. "9/11 Commission Could Subpoena Oval Office Files," *New York Times,* Philip Shenon (October 26, 2003)

213. "9/11 Whistleblower Rowley on Mueller's History of 'Cover-ups,'" *Accuracy.Org* (May 18, 2017)

214. "Crime and Punishment." *Harper's Magazine,* Andrew Cockburn (October 2017).

215. *Id.*

216. *Id.*

217. *Id.*

218. *Id.*

219. *Id.*

220. *Id.*

221. *Id.*

222. *Id.*

223. *Id.*

224. *Id.*

225. *Id.*

226. "9/11 Commission Says U.S. Agencies Slow Its Inquiry," *New York Times,* Philip Shenon (July 9, 2003)

227. "Mueller's History of Cover-Ups," *Dig Within,* Kevin Ryan (April 8, 2018).

228. Jon Kreindler, Interview with *InfoWars* (July 7, 2018)

229. "Former senator: Release the uncensored truth about 9/11," *The Washington Post,* Senator Bob Graham (retired) (May 11, 2016)

230. "Why a Special Counsel Should Be Appointed to Investigate Robert Mueller." *Strategic Culture Foundation,* Eric Zuesse (July 11, 2017).

231. "Robert Mueller Is an Amoral Legal Assassin: He Will Do His Job If You Let Him." *LaRouchePAC,* Barbara Boyd (September 27, 2017).

232. *Id.*

233. "29 Pages Revealed: Corruption, Crime and Cover-up Of 9/11." *The Huffington Post,* Kristen Breitweiser (July 17, 2017).

234. "Robert Mueller Is an Amoral Legal Assassin: He Will Do His Job If You Let Him." *LaRouchePAC*, Barbara Boyd (September 27, 2017).

235. "Al Qaeda Flying Planes Into the World Trade Center and Pentagon Was Foreseeable." *Washington's Blog*, (June 14, 2011). (emphasis in original)

Chapter 7 *Anthrax*

236. "Tales of Addiction, Anxiety, Ranting," *Washingtonpost.com*, Amy Goldstein, Nelson Hernandez, Anne Hull (August 6, 2008)

237. "World's Top Anthrax Experts Say the Killer Anthrax Was Weaponized," *WashingtonsBlog*, (Sept. 2008).

238. *Id.*

239. "FBI's Theory on Anthrax is Doubted," *The Washington Post*, Guy Gugliotta and Gary Matsumoto (October 28, 2002).

240. *Id.* (emphasis added)

241. "Bruce Ivins Wasn't the Anthrax Culprit." *The Wall Street Journal*, Richard Spertzel (August 5, 2008). (emphasis in Original)

242. "HEAD of the FBI's Anthrax Investigation Says the Whole Thing Was a SHAM," *WashingtonsBlog* (April 17, 2015) (emphasis added)

243. "World's Top Anthrax Experts Say the Killer Anthrax Was Weaponized," *WashingtonsBlog*, (September 2008).

244. "HEAD of the FBI's Anthrax Investigation Says the Whole Thing Was a SHAM," *WashingtonsBlog* (April 17, 2015)

245. "The 2001 Anthrax Deception: the Case for a Domestic Conspiracy," *Clarity Press, Inc.*, Graeme MacQueen (2014).

246. "National Academies of Science: FBI Failed to Prove Anthrax Claims," *WashingtonsBlog* (February 15, 2011)

247. "Scientists Question FBI Probe on Anthrax," *Washingtonpost.com,* Joby Warrick, Marilyn W. Thompson and Aaron C. Davis (August 3, 2008)

248. "National Academies of Science: FBI Failed to Prove Anthrax Claims," *WashingtonsBlog* (February 15, 2011)

249. "A NATION CHALLENGED: THE INQUIRY; Experts See F.B.I. Missteps Hampering Anthrax Inquiry." *The New York Times,* William Broad, David Johnston, Judith Miller, and Paul Zielbauer (November 9, 2001).

Chapter 8 *Weapons of Mass Destruction*

250. "Costs of War Project," Watson Institute for International Studies at Brown University (March 14, 2013).

251. "How Many U.S. Soldiers Were Wounded in Iraq? Guess Again.", *Huffington Post,* Dan Froomkin (December 30, 2011; Updated February 29, 2012)

252. "Iraq War Costs U.S. More than $2 Trillion: Study." *Reuters World News,* Daniel Trotta (March 14, 2013).

253. "No, Really, George W. Bush Lied about WMDs." *Vox,* Dylan Matthews (July 9, 2016).

254. "Mueller: 'Enemy Is Far from Defeated'." *CNN,* (February 11, 2003).

Chapter 9 *The Surveillance State*

255. "Robert Mueller: Gone Fishing." *Consortiumnews.com,* Ray McGovern and Bill Binney (May 1, 2018).

256. Complaint Filed with Inspector General of the Department of Justice, filed by Sander Hicks (October 11, 2007).

257. "Who Killed Dr. Graham?" *sanderhicks.com,* Sander Hicks.

258. "The Strange Death of Dr. David M. Graham." *YES! Weekly,* Jordan Green (October 23, 2007).

259. "Who Killed Dr. Graham?" *sanderhicks.com.,* Sander Hicks.

260. *Id.*
261. "The Strange Death of Dr. David M. Graham." *YES! Weekly*, Jordan Green (October 23, 2007).
262. "Crime and Punishment." *Harper's Magazine*, Andrew Cockburn (October 2017).
263. Complaint Filed with Inspector General of the Department of Justice, filed by Sander Hicks (October 11, 2007).
264. Complaint Filed with Inspector General of the Department of Justice, filed by Sander Hicks (October 11, 2007).
265. "The Strange Death of Dr. David M. Graham." *YES! Weekly*, Jordan Green (October 23, 2007).
266. "The Strange Death of Dr. David M. Graham." *YES! Weekly*, Jordan Green (October 23, 2007).
267. *Id.*
268. *Id.*
269. *Id.*
270. *Id.*
271. *Id.*
272. *Id.*
273. Complaint Filed with Inspector General of the Department of Justice, filed by Sander Hicks (October 11, 2007); "The Strange Death of Dr. David M. Graham." *YES! Weekly*, Jordan Green (October 23, 2007).
274. Complaint Filed with Inspector General of the Department of Justice, filed by Sander Hicks (October 11, 2007).
275. "The Strange Death of Dr. David M. Graham." *YES! Weekly*, Jordan Green (October 23, 2007).
276. *Id.*
277. *Id.*
278. Complaint Filed with Inspector General of the Department of Justice, filed by Sander Hicks (October 11, 2007).
279. "The Strange Death of Dr. David M. Graham." *YES! Weekly*, Jordan Green (October 23, 2007).
280. *Id.*
281. "Who Killed Dr. Graham?" *sanderhicks.com*, Sander Hicks.

282. Complaint Filed with Inspector General of the Department of Justice, filed by Sander Hicks (October 11, 2007).

283. "Who Killed Dr. Graham?" *sanderhicks.com,* Sander Hicks.

284. Complaint Filed with Inspector General of the Department of Justice, filed by Sander Hicks (October 11, 2007).

285. *Id.*

286. *Id.*

287. *Id.*

288. "The Strange Death of Dr. David M. Graham." *YES! Weekly*, Jordan Green (October 23, 2007).

289. *Id.*

290. *Id.*

291. *Id.* (emphasis added)

292. *Id.*

293. "The Strange Death of Dr. David M. Graham." *YES! Weekly*, Jordan Green (October 23, 2007).

294. *Id.*

295. Complaint Filed with Inspector General of the Department of Justice, filed by Sander Hicks (October 11, 2007).

296. Complaint Filed with Inspector General of the Department of Justice, filed by Sander Hicks (October 11, 2007).

297. "Robert Mueller Is an Amoral Legal Assassin: He Will Do His Job If You Let Him." *LaRouchePAC*, Barbara Boyd (September 27, 2017).

298. "Gonzales Hospital Episode Detailed." *The Washington Post*, Dan Eggen and Paul Kane (May 16, 2007). (emphasis added)

299. "Robert Mueller Is an Amoral Legal Assassin: He Will Do His Job If You Let Him." *LaRouchePAC*, Barbara Boyd (September 27, 2017).

300. "Robert Mueller's Forgotten Surveillance Crime Spree." *The Hill*, James Bovard (January 30, 2018).

301. *Id.*

302. *Id.*

303. *Id.*

304. *Id.*

305. *Id.*
306. "Robert Mueller: Gone Fishing." *Consortiumnews.com*, Ray McGovern and Bill Binney (May 1, 2018).
307. *Id.*
308. "Robert Mueller's Forgotten Surveillance Crime Spree." *The Hill*, James Bovard (January 30, 2018).
309. *Id.*
310 "The FBI's Secret Scrutiny." *The Washington Post,* Barton Gellman (November 6, 2005).
311. "Robert Mueller's Forgotten Surveillance Crime Spree." *The Hill*, James Bovard (January 30, 2018).
312. "Judge Invalidates Patriot Act Provisions." *The Washington Post*, Dan Eggen (September 7, 2007).
313. "Federal Judge Strikes Down NSA's Bulk Metadata Program,'" *Washington's Blog*, (December 16, 2013).
314. "FBI Director, Congressional Leaders Defend Data Mining," *CNN*, Tom Cohen (June 15, 2013).
315. *Id.*
316. "Robert Mueller's Forgotten Surveillance Crime Spree." *The Hill*, James Bovard (January 30, 2018).
317. *Id.*
318. *Id.*
319. *Id.*
320. *Id.*
321. *Id.*
322. Statement of Robert S. Mueller, III before the Senate Judiciary Committee (June 19, 2013)
323. "Robert Mueller Is an Amoral Legal Assassin: He Will Do His Job If You Let Him." *LaRouchePAC*, Barbara Boyd (September 27, 2017).
324. *Id.*
325. Testimony of Robert Mueller to House Judiciary Committee, (June 13, 2013).
326. *Id.* (emphasis added)
327. *Id.*
328. *Id.*

329.	Chris Farrell of Judicial Watch, Interview with *InfoWars* (July 7, 2018)

330.	"FBI Director: Surveillance Programs Might Have Prevented 9/11." *CBS News*, Lucy Madison (June 13, 2013).

331.	"Robert Mueller Just Wants Your Metadata," *The Guardian*, Marcy Wheeler (June 13, 2013).

Chapter 10 *The War on Donald Trump*

332.	*See, e.g.,* "Killing the Deep State: The Fight to Save President Trump," *Humanix Books*, Jerome Corsi (2018), at p. 5, 6, 10, 19, 21.

333.	*Id.* at ix.

334.	*Id.* at x.

335.	*Id.* at x.

336.	*Id.* at x.

337.	*Id.* at x.

338.	*Id.* at x.

339.	The Inaugural Address of President Donald J. Trump, (January 20, 2017).

340.	*Id.* at xi.

341.	"Killing the Deep State: The Fight to Save President Trump," *Humanix Books*, Jerome Corsi (2018), at xi.

342.	Interview of Mollie Hemingway, "Tucker Carlson Tonight," *Fox News* (May 16, 2018).

343.	"Killing the Deep State: The Fight to Save President Trump," *Humanix Books*, Jerome Corsi (2018), at p. 29.

344.	*Id.* at p. 9.

345.	*Id.* at p. 58-59, 62-64.

346.	*Id.* at p. 97-117.

347.	*Id.* at p. 100-01.

348.	*Id.* at p. 104.

349.	*Id.* at p. 101-03.

350.	*Id* at p. 98.

351.	*Id.* at p. 98.

352. *Id. at p. 106.*
353. *Id.* at p. 107.
354. *Id.* at p. 8-9.
355. *Id.* at p. 8.
356. *Id.* at p. 4-5.
357. *Id.* at p. 6.
358. *Id.* at p. 8.
359. *Id.* at p. 8.
360. Interview of James Clapper, Director of National Intelligence, *NBC News,* (March 5, 2017).
361. "Killing the Deep State: The Fight to Save President Trump," *Humanix Books*, Jerome Corsi (2018), at p. 61.
362. "Stopping Robert Mueller to Protect Us All." *The Hill,* Mark Penn (May 22, 2018).
363. "Killing the Deep State: The Fight to Save President Trump," *Humanix Books*, Jerome Corsi (2018) at xi, 29.
364. *See,* "Killing the Deep State: The Fight to Save President Trump," *Humanix Books*, Jerome Corsi (2018), at p. xi, 29; *See also,* "Robert Mueller: Gone Fishing." *Consortiumnews.com*, Ray McGovern and Bill Binney (May 1, 2018).
365. *Id.*
366. "Robert Mueller: Gone Fishing." *Consortiumnews.com*, Ray McGovern and Bill Binney (May 1, 2018).
367. "Robert Mueller Is a Communist Dupe Leading a Conspiracy to Overthrow a US Presidential Election." *The Hypnotic Communist*, Calvin W. Fields, III (January 29, 2018).
368. "Robert Mueller: Gone Fishing." *Consortiumnews.com*, Ray McGovern and Bill Binney (May 1, 2018).
369. *Id.*
370. *Id.*
371. *Id.*
372. *Id.*
373. *Id.*
374. 25th Amendment to the United States Constitution.

375. *See* "Killing the Deep State: The Fight to Save President Trump," *Humanix Books*, Jerome Corsi (2018), at p. xi, 29.

376. *See*, e.g., "Robert Mueller: Gone Fishing." *Consortiumnews.com*, Ray McGovern and Bill Binney (May 1, 2018).

377. "Former Mueller deputy on Trump: 'Government is going to kill this guy,'" *The Hill,* Joe Concha, (August 11, 2017) (emphasis added)

378. *Id.* (emphasis added)

379. "Killing the Deep State: The Fight to Save President Trump," *Humanix Books*, Jerome Corsi (2018), at p. 29.

380. *Id.* at p. 37.

Chapter 11 *A Tale of Two Muellers*

381. "Robert Mueller Has No Comment." *POLITICO,* Darren Samuelsohn (October 2, 2017).

382. *Id.*

383. "Mueller: Godfather of the Surveillance State," *InfoWars*, Jon Bowne (July 8, 2018).

Bibliography

ABC News. "Bush Warned of Hijackings Before 9-11." ABC News Network, 15 May 2002, abcnews.go.com/US/story?id=91651&page=1.

"Al Qaeda Flying Planes Into the World Trade Center and Pentagon Was Foreseeable." Washington's Blog, 14 June 2011, washingtonsblog.com/2011/06/al-qaeda-flying-planes-into-the-world-trade-center-and-pentagon-was-foreseeable.html.

Albright, Syd. "Idaho's Tragedy at Ruby Ridge." The Coeur D'Alene Press - Local News, 13 Sept. 2014, www.cdapress.com/archive/article-44130b08-6a05-582f-b64d-839d98c45aa8.html.

Anderson, Erick. "FLIGHT 103: The OTHER Story." 8 June 1999, www.fatdawg.com/flight.html.

Ashton, John, and Ian Ferguson. "Cover-up of Convenience: the Hidden Scandal of Lockerbie." Mainstream, 2002.

Associated Press. "Ruby Ridge: 20 Years Later, Randy Weaver's Daughter Lives in Peace." PennLive.com, 22 Aug. 2016, www.pennlive.com/midstate/index.ssf/2012/08/ruby_ridge_20_years_later.html.

Associated Press. "Scottish Leader Hits Back at FBI Director Robert Mueller on Criticism over Lockerbie Bomber Release - NY Daily News." New York Daily News, 23 Aug. 2009, www.nydailynews.com/news/world/scottish-leader-hits-back-fbi-director-robert-mueller-criticism-lockerbie-bomber-release-article-1.396306.

Boeri, David. "The Murder Case That Never Ends, The Crime That Keeps On Giving." *WBUR News*, 30 June 2010, www.wbur.org/news/2010/06/30/louis-greco.

Bovard, James. "Robert Mueller's Forgotten Surveillance Crime Spree." The Hill, 30 Jan. 2018, thehill.com/opinion/criminal-justice/371206-robert-muellers-forgotten-surveillance-crime-spree.

Boyd, Barbara. "Robert Mueller Is an Amoral Legal Assassin: He Will Do His Job If You Let Him." *LaRouchePAC*, 27 Sept. 2017, larouchepac.com/20170927/robert-mueller-amoral-legal-assassin-he-will-do-his-job-if-you-let-him.

Breitweiser, Kristen. "29 Pages Revealed: Corruption, Crime and Cover-up Of 9/11." The Huffington Post, HuffingtonPost.com, 17 July 2017, www.huffingtonpost.com/kristen-breitweiser/29-pages-revealed-corrupt_b_11033068.html.

Brewer, Gordon. "Lockerbie Trial: An Intelligence Operation?" BBC, 5 Oct. 2007, i-p-o.org/IPO-nr-Lockerbie-5Oct07.htm.

Broad, William J., et al. "A NATION CHALLENGED: THE INQUIRY; Experts See F.B.I. Missteps Hampering Anthrax Inquiry." The New York Times, The New York Times, 9 Nov. 2001, www.nytimes.com/2001/11/09/us/nation-challenged-inquiry-experts-see-fbi-missteps-hampering-anthrax-inquiry.html.

Carter, Sara. "Questions Still Surround Robert Mueller's Boston Past." Sara A. Carter, 19 Mar. 2018, saraacarter.com/questions-still-surround-robert-muellers-boston-past/.

Carter, Sara. "Robert Mueller, Andrew Weissmann, the FBI and the Mob." Sara A. Carter, 22 Mar. 2018, saraacarter.com/robert-mueller-andrew-weissmann-the-fbi-and-the-mob/.

Clark, Steven. "REPORT ON IDENTIFICATION PROCEDURES: Abdelbaset Ali Mohmed Al-Megrahi v. H.M. Advocate." Megrahimystory.net, 18 Dec. 2008, www.megrahimystory.net/downloads/Professor%20Steve%2 0Clark's%20report%2018%2012%2008.pdf.

CNN Library. "September 11 Hijackers Fast Facts." CNN, Cable News Network, 2 Aug. 2018, www.cnn.com/2013/07/27/ us/september-11th-hijackers-fast-facts/index.html.

"Coalition Letter to the House Committee on Oversight and Government Reform on Criminal Activities by the Federal Government." Polybius at The Clickto Network, Fox News, 31 Oct. 2007, web.archive.org/web/20071031085021 /http://www.libertycoalition.net/state-secrets-privelage/ coalition-letter-to-the-house-committee-on-oversight-and-government-reform-on-criminal-activities-by-the.

Cockburn, Andrew. "Crime and Punishment." Harper's Magazine, Oct. 2017, harpers.org/archive/2017/10/crime-and-punishment-4/.

Coelho, Courtney. "Estimated Cost of Iraq War Is 190,000 Lives and $2.2 Trillion." 'Costs of War' Project, Watson Institute International and Public Affairs at Brown University, 14 Mar. 2003, news.brown.edu/articles/2013/03/warcosts.

Cohen, Tom. "FBI Director, Congressional Leaders Defend Data Mining - CNNPolitics." CNN, Cable News Network, 15 June 2013, www.cnn.com/2013/06/13/politics/nsa-congress-mueller/index.html.

Coile, Zachary. "Another Dot That Didn't Get Connected / Newsweek Report: CIA Dropped Ball on Hijackers." SFGate, San Francisco Chronicle, 29 Jan. 2012, www.sfgate.com/news/article/Another-dot-that-didn-t-get-connected-Newsweek-2814480.php.

"Complete 9/11 Timeline." Context, www.historycommons.org/timeline.jsp?timeline=complete_911_timeline&investigations%3A_a_detailed_look=pentagon.

Computer Weekly. "Bill Binney, the 'Original' NSA Whistleblower, on Snowden, 9/11 and Illegal Surveillance." The Houston Free Thinkers, 18 Sept. 2014, thehoustonfreethinkers.com/bill-binney-the-original-nsa-whistleblower-on-snowden-911-and-illegal-surveillance/.

Concha, Joe. "Former Mueller Deputy on Trump: 'Government Is Going to Kill This Guy'." TheHill, The Hill, 11 Aug. 2017, thehill.com/homenews/media/346171-former-mueller-deputy-on-trump-government-is-going-to-kill-this-guy.

"Context of 'January 10, 2003: Government Employees Responsible for 9/11 Failures Are Rewarded and Promoted'." Context,www.historycommons.org/context.jsp?item=a120402promotions.

Corsi, Jerome R. "Killing the Deep State: The Fight to Save President Trump," Humanix Books, 2018.

Crawford, John. The Lockerbie Incident: a Detective's Tale. Trafford, 2002.

Cullen, Kevin. "A Lingering Question for the FBI's Director." The Boston Globe, 24 July 2011, archive.boston.com/news/local/massachusetts/articles/2011/07/24/a_lingering_question_for_the_fbis_director/.

Davey, Monica, and Ray Quintanilla. "FBI Examines Student Rolls in Terrorist Hunt." Chicagotribune.com, 19 Sept. 2001, www.chicagotribune.com/chi-0109190247sep19-story.html.

De Braeckeleer, Ludwig. "Tehran Hands Over the Remaining Funds to Jibril PFLP-GC - OhmyNews International." OhmyNews International, 31 Dec. 2008, english.ohmynews.com/articleview/article_view.asp?no=384 534&rel_no=1.

Eggen, Dan. "Judge Invalidates Patriot Act Provisions." The Washington Post, 7 Sept. 2007, www.washingtonpost .com/wpdyn/content/article/2007/09/06/AR2007090601438. html.

Eggen, Dan, and Amy Goldstein. "FBI Names 19 Men as Suspected Hijackers." The Washington Post, 16 Sept. 2001, www.washingtonpost.com/archive/politics/2001/09/16/fbi-names-19-men-as-suspected-hijackers/84338fad-9853-464a-846b-00e9660ad62c/?utm_term=.50d79af5a957.

Eggen, Dan, and Paul Kane. "Gonzales Hospital Episode Detailed." The Washington Post, 16 May 2007, www.washingtonpost.com/wp-dyn/content/article/2007/05/15/AR2007051500864.html.

Eichenwald, Kurt. "The Deafness Before the Storm." The New York Times, 11 Sept. 2012, www.nytimes.com/2012 /09/11/opinion/the-bush-white-house-was-deaf-to-9-11-warnings.html.

Emerson, Steven. "PanAm Scam." American Journalism Review, Sept. 1992, ajrarchive.org/article.asp?id=1314.

"FBI Director Mueller Was at Center of Alleged BCCI Coverup in 1991." Black Listed News, May 2009, www.black listednews.com/article/4304/fbi-director-mueller-was-at-center-of-alleged-bcci-coverup-in.html.

"Federal Judge Strikes Down NSA's Bulk Metadata Program: 'I Cannot Imagine a More 'Indiscriminate' and 'Arbitrary Invasion' Than This Systematic and High-Tech Collection and Retention of Personal Data On Virtually Every Single Citizen.'" Washington's Blog, 16 Dec. 2013, washingtonsblog.com/2013/12/federal-judge-imagine-indiscriminate-arbitrary-invasion-systematic-high-tech-collection-retention-personal-data-virtua.html.

Ferrell, Jeff. "Who Killed Dr. David Graham? Complaint Filed with DOJ." KSLA News 12, 18 Oct. 2007, www.ksla.com/story/7229970/who-killed-dr-david-graham-complaint-filed-with-doj.

Fields III, W. Calvin. "Robert Mueller Is a Communist Dupe Leading a Conspiracy to Overthrow a US Presidential Election." The Hypnotic Communist, 29 Jan. 2018, the-hypnotic-communist.com/robert-mueller-communist-dupe-leading-conspiracy-overthrow-us-presidential-election/.

"Finally Something Democrats and Republicans Agree on: Former FBI Director Is Right Pick for Special Counsel." The Washington Post, WP Company, 17 May 2017, www.washingtonpost.com/powerpost/finally-something-democrats-and-republicans-agree-on-former-fbi-director-is-right-pick-for-special-counsel/2017/05/17/32468266-3b20-11e7-9e48-c4f199710b69_story.html?utm_term=.6a3a6595e9c0.

Flaherty, Joseph. "Arizona's Andy Biggs Co-Sponsors Resolution Demanding Robert Mueller's Removal." Phoenix New Times, 1 Dec. 2017, www.phoenixnewtimes.com/news/

andy-biggs-says-special-counsel-mueller-should-resign-9840587.

Floyd, Chris. "Bush, Bin Laden, BCCI and the 9/11 Commission." Www.counterpunch.org, Counter Punch, 12 Oct. 2015, www.counterpunch.org/2003/01/31/bush-bin-laden-bcci-and-the-9-11-commission/.

Foot, Paul. Lockerbie: the Flight from Justice. Pressdram, 2001.

Froomkin, Dan. "How Many U.S. Soldiers Were Wounded in Iraq? Guess Again." The Huffington Post, TheHuffingtonPost.com, 29 Feb. 2012, www.huffington post.com/dan-froomkin/iraq-soldiers-wounded_b_1176276.html.

Gellman, Barton. "Cover Story: Is the FBI Up to the Job 10 Years After 9/11?" Time, Time Inc., 12 May 2011, content.time.com/time/magazine/article/0,9171,2068082,00.html.

Gellman, Barton. "The FBI's Secret Scrutiny." The Washington Post, WP Company, 6 Nov. 2005, www.washingtonpost.com/wpdyn/content/article/2005/11/05/AR2005110501366.html.

Gibbons, Phil. "Whitey Bulger And The FBI: What Did Robert Mueller Know And When Did He Know It?" Washington Babylon, 5 Dec. 2017, washingtonbabylon.com/whitey-bulger-and-the-fbi-what-did-robert-mueller-know-and-when-did-he-know-it/.

Goodman, H. A. "4,486 American Soldiers Have Died in Iraq. President Obama Is Continuing a Pointless and Deadly Quagmire." The Huffington Post, 7 Dec. 2017, www.huffingtonpost.com/h-a-goodman/4486-american-soldiers-ha_b_5834592.html.

"Government: FBI's Anthrax Investigation Flawed and Inaccurate." Washington's Blog, 23 Dec. 2014, washingtonsblog.com/2014/12/government-fbis-anthrax-investigation-flawed-inaccurate.html.

Graff, Garrett M. "The Untold Story of Robert Mueller's Time in Combat." Wired, Conde Nast, 7 June 2018, www.wired.com/story/robert-mueller-vietnam/.

Green, Jordan. "The Strange Death of Dr. David M. Graham." YES! Weekly, 23 Oct. 2007, yesweekly.com/The-strange-death-of-Dr-David-M-Graham-a8588/.

Grigg, William. "The New American - Did We Know What Was Coming? - March 11, 2002." Fox News, 11 Mar. 2002, web.archive.org/web/20061205023638/http://thenewamerican.com/tna/2002/03-11-2002/vol8no05_didweknow.htm.

"HEAD of the FBI's Anthrax Investigation Says the Whole Thing Was a SHAM." Washington's Blog, 17 Apr. 2015, washingtonsblog.com/2015/04/head-fbis-anthrax investigation-calls-b-s.html.

Henderson, Dean. "Pan Am Flight 103." Left Hook, 11 Apr. 2017, hendersonlefthook.wordpress.com/2017/04/11/pan-am-flight-103/.

Herridge, Catherine. "Exposure of NSA Surveillance Draws Attention to Mueller Remark about Real Time Email Tracking." Fox News, FOX News Network, 17 June 2013, www.foxnews.com/politics/2013/06/17/exposure-nsa-surveillance-draw-attention-to-mueller-remark-about-real-time.html.

Hicks, Sander. "Treason in Shreveport." 911Truth.Org, 17 Aug. 2015, 911truth.org/treason-in-shreveport/.

Hicks, Sander. "Who Killed Dr. Graham?" Sander Hicks, www.sanderhicks.com/graham.html.

Holguin, Jaime. "Two New FBI Missteps Reported." CBS News, 2 June 2002, www.cbsnews.com/news/two-new-fbi-missteps-reported/.

Hosenball, Mark. "The Road To September 11." Newsweek, 3 May 2011, www.newsweek.com/war-terror-road-september-11-151771.

"In 1863, Capt. Charles Russell Lowell Shot His Own Soldier. Murder or Duty?" New England Historical Society, 1 Oct. 2017, www.newenglandhistoricalsociety.com/1863-capt-charles-russell-lowell-shot-soldier-murder-duty/.

"It Was Ivins, With a Flask, 200 Miles from the Site of the Crime." Shadowproof, 6 Aug. 2008, shadowproof.com/2008/08/06/it-was-ivins-with-a-flask-200-miles-from-the-site-of-the-crime/.

Jasper, William. "FBI Covering for Criminals." The New American, 22 June 1998, www.thenewamerican.com/usnews/crime/item/5787-fbi-covering-for-criminals.

Jasper, William. "Probing Mueller: What Were His Roles in Boston Mafia Murders, Uranium One, and Other FBI Scandals?" The New American, 22 Mar. 2018, www.thenewamerican.com/usnews/politics/item/28555-probing-mueller-what-were-his-roles-in-boston-mafia-murders-uranium-one-and-other-fbi-scandals.

Johnston, David. "F.B.I. Director Says Agency Blundered in Idaho Standoff." The New York Times, 20 Oct. 1995, www.nytimes.com/1995/10/20/us/fbi-director-says-agency-blundered-in-idaho-standoff.html.

Johnston, David. "Flight 103: A Solution Assembled From Fragments and Debris." The New York Times, 15 Nov. 1991, www.nytimes.com/1991/11/15/world/flight-103-a-solution-assembled-from-fragments-and-debris.html.

Johnston, David. Lockerbie: the Real Story, 1989.

Kane, Muriel. "Questions for Mr. Mueller." The Wall Street Journal, 26 June 2001, www.wsj.com/articles/SB993512706741129831.

Kenny, Jack. "'Original' NSA Whistleblower Says Home Raid Was Retribution." The New American, 29 May 2014, www.thenewamerican.com/usnews/item/18376-original-nsa-whistleblower-says-home-raid-was-retribution.

Kuzmarov, Jeremy. "The Phoenix Program Was a Disaster in Vietnam and Would Be in Afghanistan—And the NYT Should Know That." History News Network, historynewsnetwork.org/article/116462.

Landay, Jonathan. "NSA Didn't Share Key Pre-Sept. 11 Information, Sources Say." Fox News, 6 June 2002, web.archive.org/web/20020806083614/http://www.bayarea.com/mld/bayarea/3416632.htm.

Leppard, David. On the Trail of Terror: the inside Story of the Lockerbie Investigation. Cape, 1991.

Leung, Rebecca. "CIA Warned Of U.S. Attack In '95." CBS News, 21 Mar. 2004, www.cbsnews.com/news/cia-warned-of-us-attack-in-95/.

Lewis, Neil. "Man in the News; A Man Made for Law Enforcement — Robert Swan Mueller III." The New York Times, 6 July 2001, www.nytimes.com/2001/07/06/us/man-in-the-news-a-man-made-for-law-enforcement-robert-swan-mueller

Lichtblau, Eric. "Inspector General Rebukes F.B.I. Over Espionage Case and Firing of Whistle-Blower." The New York Times, The New York Times, 15 Jan. 2005, www.nytimes.com/2005/01/15/us/inspector-general-rebukes-fbi-over-espionage-case-and-firing-of.html.

Lichtblau, Eric, and Josh Meyer. "9/11: FBI's Mueller States Hijackers Had No Computers, Laptops." Microchip Implants News Articles, Dec. 2005, www.wanttoknow.info/020430latimes911hijackersnolaptops.

Limbacher, Carl. "Condoleeza Rice Warned Sept. 6 About Imminent Terror Attack." News Max, 29 May 2002, web.archive.org/web/20030218145656/http://www.newsmax.com/showinside.shtml?a=2002/5/28/231650.

MacQueen, Graeme. "The 2001 Anthrax Deception: the Case for a Domestic Conspiracy". Clarity Press, Inc., 2014.

Madison, Lucy. "FBI Director: Surveillance Programs Might Have Prevented 9/11." CBS News, 13 June 2013, www.cbsnews.com/news/fbi-director-surveillance-programs-might-have-prevented-9-11/.

Martin, Patrick. "Mounting Questions over US Anthrax Probe and Scientist's Alleged Suicide." Torture and Death in America's Prisons, World Socialist Web Site Wsws.org Published by the International Committee of the Fourth International (ICFI), 4 Aug. 2008, www.wsws.org/en/articles/2008/08/anth-a04.html.

Matsakis, Louise. "Congress Is Debating Warrantless Surveillance in the Dark." Wired, Conde Nast, 23 Dec. 2017, www.wired.com/story/section-702-warrantless-surveillance-debate/.

Matthews, Dylan. "No, Really, George W. Bush Lied about WMDs." Vox, 9 July 2016, www.vox.com/2016/7/9/12123022/george-w-bush-lies-iraq-war.

McCarthy, Tom. "NSA to Release More Information on Surveillance Programs – as It Happened." The Guardian, 13 June 2013, www.theguardian.com/world/2013/jun/13/fbi-director-mueller-senate-nsa-live.

McGovern, Ray, and Bill Binney. "Robert Mueller: Gone Fishing." Consortiumnews, 1 May 2018, consortiumnews.com/2018/05/01/robert-mueller-gone-fishing/.

Miles, Hugh. "Hugh Miles: Lockerbie: Was It Iran? Syria? All I Know Is, It Wasn't." The Independent, Independent Digital News and Media, 21 Dec. 2008, www.independent.co.uk/voices/commentators/hugh-miles-lockerbie-was-it-iran-syria-all-i-know-is-it-wasnt-the-man-in-prison-1206086.html.

"Mueller: 'Enemy Is Far from Defeated'." CNN, Cable News Network, 11 Feb. 2003, www.cnn.com/2003/ALLPOLITICS/02/11/transcripts.mueller/.

"Mueller Is Not the Man to Be Investigating the Trumpster." Meetup, 18 June 2017, ww.meetup.com/North-SeattleProgressives/messages/boards/thread/50905380/0?_cookie-check=HC0hvJZGQLF9ITx5.

"Mueller's History of Cover-Ups." Dig Within, 8 Apr. 2018, digwithin.net/2018/04/08/muellers-history/.

"National Academies of Sciences: FBI Failed to Prove Anthrax Claims." Washington's Blog, 15 Feb. 2011, washingtons blog.com/2011/02/national-academies-of-sciences-fbi-failed-to-prove-anthrax-claims.html.

Norrie, Charles. "A Tale of Three Atrocities." The Lockerbie Divide, 20 Aug. 2010, lockerbiedivide.blogspot.com/2010 /08/tale-of-three-atrocities.html.

"'OVERSIGHT OF THE FEDERAL BUREAU OF INVESTIGATION.'" Committee on the Judiciary United States Senate, Robert S. Mueller, III, 19 June 2013.

"'OVERSIGHT OF THE FEDERAL BUREAU OF INVESTIGATION.'" Committee on the Judiciary United States House of Representatives, Robert S. Mueller, III, 13 June 2013.

"Pan Am Flight 103/ Lockerbie Air Disaster Archives." Pan Am Flight 103/Lockerbie Air Disaster Archives, 2010, panam103.syr.edu/victims/pa103_v_mckee_charles.php.

"Paul Charlton Appears on Phoenix TV to Discuss Robert Mueller, Russia Probe." Steptoe & Johnson LLP, 19 May 2017, www.steptoe.com/en/news-publications/paul-charlton-appears-on-phoenix-tv-to-discuss-robert-mueller-russia-probe.html.

Pease, Lisa. "Lockerbie Doubts." Consortiumnews, 23 May 2012, consortiumnews.com/2012/05/23/lockerbie-doubts/.

Peirce, Gareth. "The Framing of Al-Megrahi: The Death of Justice." London Review of Books, 20 May 2012, www.lrb.co.uk/v31/n18/gareth-peirce/the-framing-of-al-megrahi.

Penn, Mark. "Stopping Robert Mueller to Protect Us All." The Hill, 22 May 2018, thehill.com/opinion/judiciary/388549-stopping-robert-mueller-to-protect-us-all.

Rayner, Gordon. "Lockerbie Bombing: CIA Believes 'to a Man' That Iran Carried out Attack on Pan Am Flight 103, Says Former Agent." The Telegraph, 11 Mar. 2014, www.telegraph.co.uk/news/uknews/terrorism-in-the-uk/106 88412/Lockerbie-bombing-CIA-believes-to-a-man-that-Iran-carried-out-attack-on-Pan-Am-Flight-103-says-former-agent.html.

Rayner, Gordon. "Lockerbie Bombing 'Was Work of Iran, Not Libya' Says Former Spy." The Telegraph, 10 Mar. 2014, www.telegraph.co.uk/news/uknews/terrorism-in-the-uk/10688067/Lockerbie-bombing-was-work-of-Iran-not-Libya-says-former-spy.html.

"Robert Mueller: The Old Fixer Is Back In Town." The Millennium Report, 31 May 2018, themillenniumreport .com/2017/05/robert-mueller-the-old-fixer-is-back-in-town/.

Roberts, Joel. "9/11 Chair: Attack Was Preventable." CBS News, 17 Dec. 2003, www.cbsnews.com/news/9-11-chair-attack-was-preventable/.

Romm, Tony, et al. "Mueller: Broaden Surveillance Powers." POLITICO, 20 June 2013, www.politico.com/story /2013 /06/fbis-robert-mueller-help-needed-to-keep-criminals-from-going-dark-093055.

Rowan, Roy. "Pan Am 103 Why Did They Die?" Time, Time Inc., 24 June 2001, content.time.com/time/magazine/article /0,9171,159523,00.html.

Rowley, Coleen. "9/11 Whistleblower Rowley on Mueller's History of 'Cover-up.'" AccuracyOrg, 18 May 2017, accuracy.org/release/911-whistleblower-rowley-on-muellers-history-of-cover-up/.

Ryan, Kevin. "Mueller's History of Cover-Ups." Dig Within, 8 Apr. 2018, digwithin.net/2018/04/08/muellers-history/.

Safire, William. "Essay; B.C.C.I.: Justice Delayed." The New York Times, 25 July 1991, www.nytimes.com/1991/07/25/ opinion/essay-bcci-justice-delayed.html.

Samuelsohn, Darren, et al. "Robert Mueller Has No Comment." POLITICO, 2 Oct. 2017, www.politico.com/story/ 2017 /10/02/robert-mueller-russia-probe-secret-243345.

"Sandia National Laboratories Test Exonerates Ivins." Washington's Blog, 25 Feb. 2009, washingtonsblog .com/2009/02/sandia-national-laboratories-test-exonerates-ivins.html.

Schwartz, Ian. "Former Mueller Deputy on Trump: Deep State, 'Government Is Going To Kill This Guy.'" RealClearPolitics, 12 Aug. 2017, www.realclearpolitics.com/ video/2017/08/12/former_mueller_deputy_phil_mudd_trump _deep_state_government_kill_this_guy.html.

"Senator: 'There Are No More Excuses for Avoiding an Independent Review and Assessment of How the FBI Handled Its Investigation in the Anthrax Case.'" Washington's Blog, 16 Feb. 2011, washingtonsblog .com/2011/02/senator-there-are-no-more-excuses-for-avoiding-an-independent-review-and-assessment-of-how-the-fbi-handled-its-investigation-in-the-anthrax-case.html.

"Senators Question 'Phoenix Memo' Author." CNN, Cable News Network, 21 May 2002, www.cnn.com/2002/US/05/21 /phoenix.memo/index.html.

Shenon, Philip. "TRACES OF TERRORISM: THE WARNINGS; F.B.I. Knew for Years About Terror Pilot Training." The New York Times, 18 May 2002, www.nytimes.com

/2002/05/18/us/traces-of-terrorism-the-warnings-fbi-knew-for-years-about-terror-pilot-training.html.

Smith, Sam. "Anthrax Case: Ivins Was a Democrat Yet Target Victims Were Liberals." Undernews, 5 Aug. 2008, prorev.com/2008/08/anthrax-case-ivins-was-democrat-yet.html.

Spertzel, Richard. "Bruce Ivins Wasn't the Anthrax Culprit." The Wall Street Journal, 5 Aug. 2008, www.wsj.com/articles/SB121789293570011775.

Staff. "Ashcroft Flying High." CBS News, CBS Interactive, 26 July 2001, www.cbsnews.com/news/ashcroft-flying-high/.

Staff. "Brother of 9/11 Victim Claims US Orchestrated the Atrocity." Daily Mail Online, Associated Newspapers, 12 Sept. 2017, www.dailymail.co.uk/news/article-4867124/9-11-conspiracy-theories-persist-16-years-atrocity.html.

Staff. "Bin Laden Family Evacuated." *CBS News*, CBS Interactive, 30 Sept. 2001, www.cbsnews.com/news/bin-laden-family-evacuated/.

Staff. "The TOP 40 Reasons to Doubt the Official Story." 911Truth.Org, 16 May 2006, 911truth.org/top-40-reasons-doubt-offical-story/.

Starmann, Ray. "13 Shocking Facts About Special Prosecutor Robert Mueller." Washington's Blog, 2 Nov. 2017, washingtonsblog.com/2017/11/10-shocking-facts-special-prosecutor-robert-mueller.html.

Stich, Rodney. "Bombing of Pan Am Flight 103 Over Lockerbie: the Truth!" LinkedIn, 30 Aug. 2014, www.linkedin.com/pulse/20140830003751-29817943-bombing-of-pan-am-flight-103-over-lockerbie-the-truth/.

Stoll, Ira. "Mueller's Mediocrity Makes Him Into A Star By Washington Standards." New Boston Post, 8 June 2017, newbostonpost.com/2017/06/08/muellers-mediocrity-makes-him-into-a-star-by-washington-standards/.

Swire, Dr. Jim, and Peter Biddulph. "Lockerbietruth.com." Our Book: Lockerbie, www.lockerbietruth.com/p/our-book.html.

"The BCCI Affair - 7 BCCI in the United States - Part Two Acquisition, Consolidation, and Consequences." Contra Report, fas.org/irp/congress/1992_rpt/bcci/07later.htm.

"The Inaugural Address." The White House, The United States Government, 20 Jan. 2018, www.whitehouse.gov/briefings-statements/the-inaugural-address/.

"The Republican Mother." *Meet Your Elites: Robert Mueller*, 13 Mar. 2012, therepublicanmother.blogspot.com/2012/03 /meet-your-elites-robert-mueller.html.

Trotta, Daniel. "Iraq War Costs U.S. More than $2 Trillion: Study." Reuters, Thomson Reuters, 14 Mar. 2013, www.reuters.com/article/us-iraq-war-anniversary-idUSBRE92D0PG20130314.

Unger, Craig. "After 9/11: the Saudis Who Slipped Away." Los Angeles Times, 11 Apr. 2004, articles.latimes .com/2004/apr/11/opinion/oe-unger11.

"US Civil Liberties." Context of 'June 9, 2005: Bush Again Claims All Surveillance Done with Court Warrants, Former AT&T Engineer Disputes Claim', www.historycommons .org/timeline.jsp?civilliberties_surveillance=civilliberties_ns a_wiretapping&printerfriendly=true&timeline=civilliberties.

Van Buren, Peter. "The New Surveillance State and the Old Perjury Trap." The American Conservative, 7 Mar. 2018, www.theamericanconservative.com/articles/the-new-surveillance-state-and-the-old-perjury-trap/.

Vulliamy, Ed, and Jason Burke. "Bush Knew of Terrorist Plot to Hijack US Planes." The Guardian, Guardian News and Media, 19 May 2002, www.theguardian.com/world/2002/may/19/terrorism.september11.

Walter, Jess, and Dean Miller. "FBI Punishes 12 Agents But Sharpshooter Who Killed Vicki Weaver Gets Off Scot-Free." Spokesman.com, The Spokesman-Review, 7 Jan. 1995, www.spokesman.com/stories/1995/jan/07/fbi-punishes-12-agents-but-sharpshooter-who/.

Weiner, Tim. "Robert Komer, 78, Figure in Vietnam, Dies." The New York Times, The New York Times, 12 Apr. 2000, www.nytimes.com/2000/04/12/world/robert-komer-78-figure-in-vietnam-dies.html.

West, Ronald. "On FBI's Comey." Ronald Thomas West, 10 May 2017, ronaldthomaswest.com/tag/bcci/.

Wheeler, Marcy. "Robert Mueller Just Wants Your Metadata | Marcy Wheeler." The Guardian, Guardian News and Media, 13 June 2013, www.theguardian.com/commentisfree/2013/jun/13/robert-mueller-metadata.

Whitaker, Brian, et al. "G8 Summit May Have Been Bin Laden Target." The Guardian, Guardian News and Media, 27 Sept. 2001,www.theguardian.com/world/2001/sep/27/globalisation.afghanistan.

Wilson, Jason. "Ruby Ridge, 1992: the Day the American Militia Movement Was Born." The Guardian, Guardian News and Media, 26 Aug. 2017, www.theguardian.com/usnews/2017/aug/26/ruby-ridge-1992-modern-american-militia-charlottesville.

"World's Top Anthrax Experts Say The Killer Anthrax Was Weaponized" Washington's Blog, Sept. 2008, georgewashington2.blogspot.com/2008/09/worlds-top-anthrax-experts-say-killer.html.

Worthington, Rogers. "Next Siege Probe For Congress: Idaho." Chicago Tribune, 6 Aug. 1995, articles.chicagotribune.com /1995-08-06/news/9508060272_1_randy-weaver-ruby-ridge-vicki-weaver.

Yost, Pete. "FBI Director Defends Surveillance Programs." BostonGlobe.com, The Boston Globe, 14 June 2013, www.bostonglobe.com/news/nation/2013/06/14/fbi-director-defends-surveillance-programs/09QlIW4PjBTiyEWiQIBI6H/story.html.

Zuesse, Eric. "Why a Special Counsel Should Be Appointed to Investigate Robert Mueller." Strategic Culture Foundation, 11 July 2017, www.strategic-culture.org/news/2017 /11/07/why-special-counsel-should-be-appointed-investigate-robert-mueller.html.